Contents

Acknowledgements		**4**
Foreword		**5**
Colin Challen MP		
Executive summary		**7**
1	**Introduction**	**11**
2	**The climate change challenge**	**13**
3	**Research design**	**28**
4	**Results and findings**	**43**
	Pursuing the target	43
	Whole market progress	53
	Improvement over time	57
	The nature of potential	60
	Potential over years	66
	Value for money	68
	Meeting targets	70
	Expert versus local view	73
	Politial viablility	75
	Trading and cost-effectiveness	76
5	**Conclusions and recommendations**	**81**
Appendix 1	Contributors	**89**
Appendix 2	Simulation timetable	**90**
Appendix 3	Returns form	**91**
Appendix 4	Example feedback email	**92**
Appendix 5	Analyst's bulletins	**94**
Appendix 6	Carbon credit prices	**98**
Appendix 7	Complete list of suggested actions	**100**
Appendix 8	Domestic microgeneration and planning	**119**
Partners		**130**

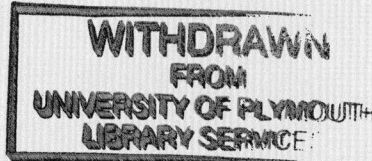

Acknowledgements

The report is the result of a period of intensive research that relied on the commitment of a small number of local officers and sustainability experts. Without their time, enthusiasm and knowledge this report would not have been possible. As a result, I am extremely grateful to all those who made this work possible.

I would also like to thank the sponsors of this project, Kirklees Council and Serco. Their financial support and intellectual input were also essential to the process. In particular, I would like to thank Graeme Cameron, Dr Stewart Davies, Philip Hume, and Philip Webber.

Finally, I would like to thank all those at NLGN who have aided me throughout the process. I would particularly like to thank Matthew Clifton for his intellectual input and support with the research process. I would also like to thank Chris Leslie and Dick Sorabji for their support and valuable insight throughout the project. Despite this support, any errors or omissions are my own.

James MacGregor
October 2007

Foreword

This report makes a welcome contribution to the debate about how society must respond to the challenge of climate change.

The role of local authorities has long been recognised as crucial, and since the inception of Agenda 21 at the Earth Summit in 1992, many councils have striven to improve their environmental performance and awareness. Local authorities are at the cutting edge in many environmental responsibilities and functions, especially in planning, waste management, transport, housing and education to name but a few.

Over 200 local authorities have now signed up to the Nottingham Declaration, and are developing detailed climate change strategies. Others have struck out individually to reduce their carbon footprints. Woking naturally comes to mind, Merton too; but many others are innovators seeking new ways to meet the challenge.

But we know we have to go much, much further. This was acknowledged by the Prime Minister in his speech to the Labour Party Conference, when he tasked the Climate Change Commission to consider a tougher target for reducing carbon emissions than is currently proposed in the Draft Climate Change Bill. All political parties recognise that the present figure of 60 per cent is insufficient. Indeed, this report suggests that if effective actions were taken, we could reduce our carbon footprint by 60 per cent by 2019.

There is no doubt that the scale of the challenge is not only large, but immediate. It is often said that we have a window of opportunity, of perhaps 10 or 15 years, in which we must put in place – globally – measures in that period which will result in carbon emissions peaking and starting to decline. This is deemed necessary if we are to ensure we do not pass the 2°C temperature increase it is thought would take us into the territory of catastrophic climate change. Given that existing emissions - which accumulate in the atmosphere for around 100 years continue to increase - we are already committed to a temperature increase of 1.5°C.

Even at the levels we are at today, which have resulted so far in an increase of nearly 0.8°C, we are beginning to witness the impacts. Glaciers melting, the retreat of the Arctic ice cap, the acidification of the oceans – the pattern of events is following and often exceeding what climate change models predict. Climate change is also blamed for many other events, for example this year's summer floods in the UK, but the causal link is not proven. We have to observe the trends in weather patterns before drawing conclusions. Nevertheless, such events fit the likely future pattern.

Local authorities will therefore be faced with today's climate change mitigation challenge as well as tomorrow's adaptation challenge. Adaptation will be called for not only in the development of flood defences, but in social adaptation. For example, how prepared are our social services for serious heatwaves, like the one that hit Europe in 2003?

Local authority emissions trading could well be part of the answer. A soundly designed cap and trade system provides incentives for finding efficient solutions to the problem. Emissions trading, already established across 10,000 major European industrial greenhouse gas emitters is an established fact and is likely to be emulated in other regions globally. Inevitably such a system will develop and organisations and perhaps even individuals will have to be engaged with the process. Trading will always be only one part of the toolkit – we shouldn't put all our policy eggs into one basket. But it will be a significant part, and as this report shows the development of trading systems on the back of evidence based research will be crucial.

Local authorities have shown that they are up for the challenge. They are responsible for the delivery of many of the services which make society tick. This report provides a clear direction of travel, and I hope that it will succeed in intensifying activity to help us solve the climate change problem faster than we are creating it.

Colin Challen MP
Chair, All Party Parliamentary Climate Change Group

Executive summary

The planet is getting warmer and we are responsible. This report investigates the scale of local government's potential for reducing greenhouse gas emissions and examines the drivers that will encourage local authorities to take action. To avoid the worst effects of climate change, the growth in atmospheric concentrations of greenhouse gases must be reversed. Only rapid action can avoid the potentially catastrophic effects of a warmer planet[1] and local government should be a much bigger part of the solution.

This report finds that:

- if the right strategic choices are made now, local government has the potential to reach the Government's **60 per cent carbon dioxide reduction target 25 years early** by 2025;

- if just the average reductions made during the research can be met, activity led by local councils could reduce carbon dioxide emissions by over **320,000,000** tonnes in 17 years; and

- such action can have a positive political effect – **tackling climate change can in fact be electorally attractive**.

Councils across the UK have already taken action to reduce the environmental footprints of their areas. Councils use their unique range of tools to make reductions in greenhouse gas emissions. But more can be done. Councils have the potential to wield their influence across the whole locality and make large reductions.

It is still not clear how the Government will achieve its self-imposed CO_2 reduction targets. Citizens are demanding that the state do better. But tackling climate change is not easy: it is a complex challenge. Emissions trading is often mooted as a solution and there is some evidence of its potential. Local government could also play a bigger role, but until now there has been a lack of certainty of what this role would be and how much could be achieved. This report helps to bridge this gap in understanding.

---

[1] *The Stern Review*, HM Treasury, Cabinet Office, 2006

This project took an innovative and powerful approach to gathering data. The project sought to develop an understanding of local government's role well into the future, rather than simply examine past experience. Therefore, our project used an innovative inter-authority carbon trading simulation where councils were set challenging targets for reducing carbon dioxide emissions:

- council environmental officers were asked to produce new suggestions for reducing emissions while being responsible for trading credits over a simulated five year period;

- all suggestions were assessed by a **panel of experts**; and

- the simulation tested the effect of targets, competition and financial incentives on performance.

Using this methodology, the report finds that local government has a far greater potential to tackle climate change than previously assumed. If the average performance of councils that took part in the simulation can be replicated across local government, the Government's 60 per cent carbon dioxide reduction target can be met by 2025. Moreover:

- if the performance of the most successful council in our simulation could be matched, **the UK could potentially meet its 60 per cent target by 2019**; and

- in the simulation, the tougher the challenge, the better councils responded.

Based on its findings, we argue that:

- councils' potential comes from their capacity to influence local partners and citizens;

- the biggest CO_2 reductions were made by councils using their wider influence over residential and commercial actors;

- placeshaping is also the most cost-effective way of tackling climate change; and

- tackling climate change also revealed itself as a political asset – over time, the political favourability of measures grew and strong political leadership can reap electoral rewards.

The following table gives five examples of successful innovative actions taken by local authorities that participated in the simulation:

Figure 1 Examples of successful innovative actions taken by local authorities that participated in the simulation[2]

Description of CO_2 reduction action	Cost (£)	Self-assessed saving (tonnes CO_2)	Estimated political impact
Construct 14 Anaerobic Digestion plants to process organic waste, producing energy from methane on two sites in the local area, which would involve working with other local authorities, partners and influencing the behaviours of local people. The approach would include new Community Schemes, with surplus energy provided to the National Grid.	17m	1,050,000	Favourable
Personalised carbon credits for all local residents with each person allocated eight tonnes per year. The scheme would use a 'Carbon Credit Card', and have new meters installed in houses to clock up the amount of electricity used. Cars would be required to use a similar device and flights would also be included within the scheme.	13m	520,000	Unfavourable
Second year of an electricity generating scheme linked to landfill sites extended to address remaining 4m tonnes of CO_2 produced from such sites.	2.5m	500,000	Favourable
In the first year, establish five District Energy Plants run on wood chip from street trees, parks trees and residents tree waste – providing heat and water to 50 per cent of homes and businesses.	10m	480,000	Unfavourable
Energy Services Company (ESCO) managing energy requirements of developments in a local Growth Area (37,500 homes, all to be built at end of year five), funded through Third Party Financing (option for financing for the project without the authorities compromising own capital, thus leaving capital available for other priorities).	500k	375,000	Favourable

2 See Annex 6.7 for a full list of actions

To rise to the climate change challenge and realise local government's potential, the current regulatory environment needs to change.

The Government's impending, legally enforceable 60 per cent reductions by 2050 target is the benchmark, but delivery is necessary. Inter-authority trading creates powerful drivers for improvement but might be too complex for the public sector.

Instead, a **package of reforms** might replicate these drivers with less complexity:

- a portion of this CO_2 reduction target should be devolved by negotiation to each local authority and managed through Local Area Agreements;

- a new performance grant could be attached to incentivise councils to exceed their targets;

- councils that do not achieve their targets would be financially penalised – this approach would be **revenue neutral** assuming that targets are set appropriately;

- the new national Committee on Climate Change should take much greater advantage of expert local opinion and local leadership;

- local government should also report on progress to Parliament alongside Ministerial accountability for the work of central government;

- targeted training across local government could help to improve negotiation skills and competencies in the financial aspects of sustainability; and

- improved data will also be essential for local government to wield influence effectively and share best practice.

The Government should embrace the potential of local government and, together with these measures, we can to rise to the climate change challenge.

1 *Introduction*

Our planet is getting warmer. Data stretching back a century reveals a steady and gradual increase in average global temperatures. If this warming trend continues unabated, it threatens not only to fundamentally alter our environment, but to destabilise the social and economic fabric of our local communities. This level of threat means that climate change is now a local problem as much as a global phenomenon. This report investigates the potential of local leadership to deliver the necessary cuts in CO$_2$ emissions.

Until recently, the extent of the contribution of human activity to the warming trend was hotly debated. This is at least in part the nature of the phenomenon; fluctuations in global temperatures can be attributed to solar activity, volcanism, variations in the earth's orbit, and greenhouse gases in varying degrees. For some, warming was the product of natural variations. Now, this is a case rarely made. The burning of fossil fuels, deforestation and modern agriculture have together contributed to a rise in global temperatures. Citizens and businesses across the world are demanding that their governments' rise to the challenge.

As with most policy questions in the 21st century, the climate change challenge is not easily met. Greenhouse gas emissions are from numerous sources; industrial, commercial, domestic and individual. Governments who try and impose change from the top-down will likely fail; people are only willing to tolerate so much hardship in pursuit of grand objectives. Instead, governments across the world are asked to persuade everybody to change their behaviours.

The Government is preparing to give itself new legal duties to reduce emissions year-on-year. What is not yet clear is how these targets are to be reached. Existing approaches have not managed to reach even less ambitious targets. An extension of emissions trading is one possible solution; international schemes already exist. But emissions trading that involves all polluters will take a long time to develop.

---

3 As far back as 1995 the Intergovernmental Panel on Climate Change found that mean surface air temperature has increased by between about 0.3° and 0.6°C since the late nineteenth century, *IPCC Second Assessment Climate Change*, 1995

Local government offers to tackle climate change more quickly. Some councils have already blazed the trail, developing local energy generation infrastructures and reducing emissions from their own estates. Councils might also be able to influence local people and businesses to reduce their environmental footprints. This publication investigates local government's potential for reducing greenhouse gas emissions. A small number of local authorities participated in a trading simulation that created incentives to tackle climate change. The report goes on to draw conclusions from the research findings and make recommendations for policy changes at the national and local level to empower the whole of the state to meet the climate change challenge.

2 *The climate change challenge*

The state has demonstrated its commitment to tackling climate change. But much work remains to be done. A new environment offers new opportunities to create a low carbon economy. Now, the scientific case for the reality of man-made climate change is indisputable.

As Stern's work on the economics of climate change has shown,[4] the need to tackle climate change is immediate. The state is readying itself to introduce tough new legal duties to take action. But the method of rising to the climate change challenge remains elusive. Citizens are increasingly demanding new solutions. This offers new opportunities to politicians to take action. The complexity of the problem intensifies the challenge. Trading schemes might help to cater for this complexity, but the evidence is lacking. Local government's unique portfolio of powers might have the potential to have a significant affect on greenhouse gas emissions. Local government's potential merits further investigation.

The end of the debate

The link between human activity and climate change has long been debated. In 1988 the UN created the Intergovernmental Panel on Climate Change (IPCC) to provide an objective source of information about the causes of climate change. Over the last 19 years, the panel has published a series of papers analysing and summarising existing peer reviewed scientific data.

Environmentalists, campaigners and some scientists have long made the argument that two kinds of human activity will inevitably lead to rising global temperatures. The first is the burning of fossil fuels. This releases the greenhouse gases locked-up for millions of years into the atmosphere, which encourages the atmosphere to trap more heat. The second is changing the way land is used. Deforestation and modern agribusiness means have led to less vegetation to absorb greenhouse gases. Together, these processes are leading to higher atmospheric concentrations of gases that trap heat.

---

4 Sir Nicholas Stern, *Stern Review on the Economics of Climate Change*, HM Treasury, Cabinet Office (November 2006)

The panel's first report in 1990 found that gathering the data to make an unequivocal finding on the human contribution to climate change was at least a decade away.[5] In 1995, the panel concluded that the global warming trend is unlikely to be entirely natural in origin.[6] The 2001 report found that 'the Earth's climate system has demonstrably changed on both global and regional scales since the pre-industrial era, with some of these changes attributable to human activities.'[7]

The 2007 report makes the strongest link yet. It found that, 'Global atmospheric concentrations of carbon dioxide (CO_2), methane and nitrous oxide have increased markedly as a result of human activities since 1750 and now far exceed pre-industrial values'. The panel went on to conclude, with 'very high confidence'[8] that, 'the globally averaged net effect of human activities since 1750 has been one of warming.'[9] For the vast majority of the global scientific community, human-induced climate change is a reality. The scientific debate is over. But the end of this debate is the beginning of a new and more complex one. This debate will focus on how to rise to the challenge and avoid the negative impacts of climate change.

State action

In the recent past the state has taken numerous steps to improve energy efficiency, promote green energy and as a result tackle climate change through regulation and legislation. In 2000, the Government introduced the Climate Change Programme that committed to reducing greenhouse gas emissions by more than agreed at Kyoto. This has since been superseded by the 2006 programme. The UK is in the process of fully implementing EU regulations on the energy performance of buildings. The Climate Change Levy and the Landfill Tax have created incentives for energy users and waste producers to reduce their consumption. The Renewables Obligation requires energy generating companies to source a small portion of their electricity from renewable resources. The Low

5 IPCC, *First Assessment Report*, Executive Summary (1990)

6 IPCC, *Second Assessment Report, Summary for Policymakers: The Science of Climate Change* (1995), Section 4

7 IPCC, *Climate Change 2001: Synthesis Report – Summary for Policymakers*, (September 2001) p 4

8 In using this term, the authors are making an expert judgement on the correctness of the underlying science. 'Very high confidence' means that the finding has at least a 9 out of 10 chance of being correct.

9 IPCC, *IPCC Fourth Assessment Report, the Physical Science Base: Summary for Policymakers* (February 2007) p 5

Carbon Buildings Programme (LCBP) introduced grants for sustainable micro-generation infrastructure.

The Government has also established new institutions; the Energy Savings Trust and the Carbon Trust exist to encourage citizens and organisations to take part in building a local carbon economy. The Carbon Trust runs a number of sector-specific carbon management programmes aimed at helping organisations to reduce greenhouse gas emissions under their direct control.

The most ambitious element of the Government's approach has been entry into the EU Emissions Trading Scheme, the world's largest example of multi-national greenhouse gas trading. The scheme has established a framework for energy-intensive industries to buy and sell carbon credits among themselves. The scheme intends to realistically reflect the social cost of carbon and give companies financial incentive to change their behaviours.

Local government also has a long-standing role. Agenda 21, agreed at the Rio Earth Summit in 1992, required that each local authority draw up a Local Agenda 21 (LA21) strategy in consultation with local people. The Nottingham Declaration, initially made in 2000, accepts the reality of climate change and commits signatories '…to tackling the causes and effects of a changing climate,' on the locality.[10] To date, the Declaration has over 200 local authority signatories.

Many councils have taken large strides towards creating a low carbon economy. Woking Borough Council, for example, has reduced its carbon emissions from its own estate by over 70 per cent through using energy more efficiently and installing new micro-generation infrastructure over the last fifteen years. Kirklees Council has run a scheme that is now responsible for generating around five per cent of UK's solar electricity. London Borough of Merton has pioneered new planning regulations that require all major new developments to reduce expected carbon emissions by at least ten per cent by using on-site renewables. The principles of this 'Merton Rule' are being adopted across local government.

All this action has achieved some progress; between 1997 and 2005, emissions fell by about seven per cent.[11] But the Government's self-imposed targets are now

---

10 *The Nottingham Declaration on Climate Change, Revised Version* (August 2006)
11 DEFRA, *Estimated emissions of carbon dioxide (CO_2) by UNECE source category, type of fuel and end user* (January 2007)

almost certain to be missed. The proportion of energy generated from renewable sources will not reach ten per cent by 2010 or 15 per cent by 2015. Greenhouse gas emissions will not fall by 20 per cent of 1990 levels by 2010. So, despite progress, the rate of improvement is not enough. Faster progress is necessary. For the UN Intergovernmental Panel on Climate Change (IPCC), 'With current climate change mitigation policies and related sustainable development practices, global greenhouse gas emissions will continue to grow over the next few decades.'[12]

As the 'Stern Review' concluded, the pace of progress will be the deciding factor in how far we can rise to the climate change challenge. The slower the progress towards creating a low carbon economy, the greater the impact of the changing climate. Further, the longer action is delayed, the more expensive it will become. New approaches are required. To create these solutions, it is necessary to understand the nature of the challenge.

The climate change challenge

The effects of a sustained increase in the atmospheric concentration of greenhouse gases at the current rate could be dramatic. For the IPCC, it is very likely that the changes in global climate this century will be larger than the effects in the last.[13] Even if the current trend of increase does not continue and the atmospheric concentration of greenhouse gases remains constant at 2000 levels, a further warming of about 0.5°C per decade can be expected.[14] The IPCC concludes that unless action is taken global average temperatures are likely to rise by between 1.8°C and 4°C by the end of the century, sea levels are likely to rise and the oceans are likely to become more acidic. Hot extremes, heat waves and heavy precipitation will continue to become more frequent.[15]

It is not an exaggeration to say that such developments threaten the future of civilisation. Higher sea levels will flood many of the world's major population centres. Warmer seas will increase the frequency and violence of extreme weather events. But these effects are not inevitable; there remains time to change. The IPCC's scenario assumes no reduction in the atmospheric

---

[12] IPCC, *IPCC Fourth Assessment Report, Working Group III: Summary for Policymakers* (May 2007), p4 Section B.3

[13] IPCC, *IPCC Fourth Assessment Report, the Physical Science Base: Summary for Policymakers* (February 2007) p13

[14] Ibid, p12

[15] Ibid, p7

concentration of greenhouse gases from 2000 levels. As Stern found, 'There is still time to avoid the worst impacts of climate change if strong collective action starts now.'[16] The IPCC has found that concerted action can, 'offset the projected growth of global emissions or reduce emissions below current levels.'[17]

Stern has shown that, if we choose not to act, the financial impact of climate change will be equivalent to losing at least five per cent of global GDP annually. This impact would be greater than a combination of the Great Depression and both world wars. Reducing greenhouse gas production to a position where the catastrophic effects of global warming will be avoided will cost significantly less; around one per cent of global GDP annually. The Stern Review highlights that there is not a technology barrier to achieving this change. The challenge rests on whether there is the political will to catalyse changes in sustainable consumption and production across the economy by putting in place the required policy, fiscal and regulatory measures. The IPCC's most recent report draws a stark conclusion: in between ten and fifteen years global greenhouse gas emissions need to peak and decline if we are to avoid the worst effects of climate change.

The Government recognises local government's role in rising to this challenge. The Secretary of State for Environment, Food and Rural Affairs, Hilary Benn MP, recently asserted his belief in the potential of local government, saying, 'Local government is not just a partner in this fight. [It is] one of the leaders of this fight'. Adding that, 'We won't tackle climate change, or improve the environment that we all share, without local government leading the way.'[18]

Public attitudes: local variation

It is not enough that scientific and political communities recognise the impact of human activity on climate change; public attitudes and behaviours also need to change. Effective action to avoid climate change's worst effects will rely on the willingness of citizens and communities to change their behaviour. It is unlikely that the state can address a challenge on this scale without public support.

The UK's major political parties see policies aimed at tackling climate change as potential vote winners. The Labour Party has made much of its efforts to secure

---

16 Sir Nicholas Stern, *Stern Review: The Economics of Climate Change*, HM Treasury, Cabinet Office (November 2006), Full Executive Summary, p xxvii

17 IPCC, *IPCC Fourth Assessment Report, Mitigation of Climate Change: Summary for Policymakers* (February 2007)

18 Speech to Local Government Association Conference, 5 July 2007

global agreements on reducing greenhouse gas production. The Conservative Party has made its 'Vote Blue, Go Green' message a central part of its political campaigning. Zac Goldsmith's and John Gummer's report *Blueprint for a Green Economy* appears set to form a central plank of Conservative policy. The Liberal Democrats have renewed their longstanding commitment to green policies in their recent report *Zero Carbon Britain – Taking a Global Lead*. The Green Party continues to build its political popularity and grow its base of local councillors.

There is evidence that this growing political commitment is a reflection of the growing importance of environmental issues among the general public. In May 2002, only one per cent of respondents saw pollution and the environment as one of the most important issues facing the UK. By 2007, this figure had increased to 19 per cent in January, falling back to 12 per cent in April.[19] A recent poll revealed that almost three-quarters of those surveyed agreed with the statement, 'Environmental issues like climate change are very important to me and will influence how I vote at the next general election.' Also, a majority agreed with the statement, 'The government should impose higher taxes on activities that cause pollution, even if that means the end of cheap flights and driving a car becomes more expensive.'[20]

Other data shows that individuals rank climate change as second to terrorists as the biggest threat currently facing the UK. When asked what will be the greatest threat to the UK in twenty years time, climate change was ranked first. These responses were grouped by region – 63 per cent of respondents in the South East saw climate change as the biggest threat in twenty years, compared to 55 per cent in Wales and the South West and only 53 per cent in Scotland.[21] This regional variation suggests that the same policies will be received differently by the general public in different parts of the UK. What is acceptable in Dover might not be so in Fife. Policymakers are challenged to design solutions to the climate change challenge that take account of these variations.

There is also increasing social pressure to address climate change. A recent survey found that more than half of the people questioned considered unethical living less socially acceptable than drink-driving. Three quarters of respondents

---

[19] Mori Poll, *Political Monitor: Long-Terms Trends. The most Important Issues Facing Britain Today* (from September 1974 to present)

[20] Populus, *Political Parties and the Environment for The Daily Politics* (October 2006)

[21] Populus, *Nuclear Weapons Survey for More4 News* (February 2007)

said that environmental impact is one of the main topics of conversation with peers.[22] This growth in acceptance will offer opportunities for politicians to take responsibility for measures to tackle the problem to an extent unlikely even a few years ago. The time is ripe for political action.

Business responses

The growing importance of climate change to the general public is also reflected in business behaviours. The Carbon Disclosure Project is an international initiative designed to collect data on the business implications of climate change and individual companies' carbon footprints. The project aims to develop a better understanding of the role of business in tackling climate change and the potential effects on business.

Across the business sector, there is evidence of a growing awareness at both strategic and operational levels of the challenge of climate change. Leading businesses are addressing the change in future markets that might arise from the drive for a low carbon economy. For some, this means the growth of new product or service opportunities. For others, threats to supply chains that are unsustainable. For all, climate change represents a change that can be predicted and one which company boards are duty-bound to address.

UK companies are taking practical steps. Eight of the UK's leading companies are working with the Climate Group and the Government on the 'We're in this Together' initiative, which aims to influence customers' behaviour and promote environmentally friendly products. These businesses recognise that there are commercial advantages to be had from rising to the climate change challenge.

The Government is increasingly turning to the private sector as a proactive partner in rising to the climate change challenge. The Government acknowledges its need to learn from exemplary companies that are seeing through changes from boardroom strategy to shop-floor implementation. In its own supply chain, the Government now has product and service suppliers offering solutions to reducing the carbon footprint of the Government's own operations. The Sustainable Procurement Task Force identified further steps that the Government must take to allow businesses to contribute to their full potential. [23]

---

22 Survey by Tickbox.net for Norwich Union, *'Be good guilt' leads Brits to tell little green lies* (August 2007)
23 Sustainable Procurement National Action Plan, *Procuring the Future: Sustainable Procurement National Action Plan* (2006). This report outlines a series of recommendations designed to encourage the whole of the state to realise the benefits of sustainable procurement from private organisations.

Scale and scope

The nature of the problem intensifies the challenge to policymakers. If greenhouse gases came from only a few identifiable sources, it would be a relatively easy task to reduce them. But greenhouse gases come from many disparate sources:

- **road transport** (120m tonnes);

- **energy industries** (208m tonnes);

- **other industries** (99m tonnes);

- **residential** (83m tonnes); and

- **other** – mainly commercial and public sectors (46m tonnes).[24]

These classifications mask the complex patterns behind each heading. Road transport, for example, involves 33.4m registered vehicles.[25] This figure includes private cars, public transport and private haulage. It seems unlikely that any single policy can persuade all drivers and businesses that rely on the road network to change their behaviours. Similarly, even if one measure was theoretically capable of reducing emissions, it might not be acceptable to road users and businesses alike. As the IPCC has suggested, 'Changes in lifestyle and behaviour patterns can contribute to climate change mitigation across all sectors.'[26] The next wave of policy solutions is required to address the challenge in all its aspects.

A complete solution

The search for solutions that can cater for this complexity is ongoing. The Greater London Authority has set an abitious timescale to address this complex challenge. The Mayor's Climate Change Action Plan aims to reduce London carbon emissions by four per cent annually from 1990 levels, leading to a 60 per cent reduction by 2025. This will be achieved by tailoring methods of carbon reduction emissions to the four major areas of carbon production: ground

24 Department for Food, Environment and Rural Affairs, *Global Atmosphere: Carbon Dioxide Emissions by Source 1990-2005, CO₂ Equivalents* (January 2007)
25 Department for Transport, *Statistical Release on Vehicle Licensing Statistics: 2006* (March 2007)
26 IPCC, *IPCC Fourth Assessment Report, Working Group III: Summary for Policymakers* (May 2007), p17, Section C.7

transport, industry, commerce and homes. Changing behaviour will play an important role; roughly half the reduction will be delivered if just two thirds of Londoners make simple behavioural changes and put some basic energy efficiency measures in place.[27]

Central government is also constructing new approaches. The draft Climate Change Bill will set five-year, legally binding targets for reducing UK carbon emissions. The aims will be to reduce emissions by between 26 and 32 per cent by 2020, and by 60 per cent by 2050 compared with 1990 levels. Ministers will be required to report annually to Parliament on progress against these targets.

But setting demanding targets is only the beginning. It is also necessary to create new ways of reaching these targets. The immediacy of the challenge means that the state cannot again afford to fall short of its ambitions. The Act, if passed in its current form, will create a framework designed to encourage new practical solutions. A new independent Committee on Climate Change will advise the Government on how to achieve the 2050 target in the areas of carbon budgets, carbon trading schemes and appropriate balance between domestic and international action. The Government will be able to introduce new trading schemes without the need for new laws.

Emissions trading

Emissions trading seems set to become a central element of the Government's attempts to rise to the climate change challenge. New enabling powers aside, the Government is already planning to introduce a new domestic trading scheme known as the Carbon Reduction Commitment. This mandatory scheme will set new emissions caps for large organisations with electricity bills of over £500,000. Participants will receive annual financial rewards or penalties depending on their league table positions. The aim is to save 1,100 kilotonnes of CO_2 by 2020. Trading schemes like this are attractive to policymakers as they promise to create new incentives for producers of carbon to reduce their own emissions.

The Government has been exploring the potential of other trading schemes. The Department for Food, Environment and Rural Affairs (DEFRA) recently commissioned the Centre for Sustainable Energy to produce a scoping study exploring the potential of individual carbon trading. The study uncovered

---

27 Mayor of London, *Action Today to Protect Tomorrow: The Mayor's Climate Change Action Plan* (February 2007), p xvi

questions about technical feasibility and impact. It went on to construct a five-year road map for implementing individual carbon trading.[28]

Outside government, the Royal Society for the Encouragement of Arts, Manufacture and Commerce (RSA) is exploring the idea of personal carbon trading through its Carbon*Limited* project. Their investigation is based on the approach outlined by David Fleming.[29] The project is designed to lead to policy recommendations. For the RSA, there are three benefits to using a personal carbon trading framework; firstly, to show global leadership on climate change; secondly, to bring forward in time a decline in greenhouse gas emissions; and thirdly, gaining commercial advantage through carbon trading markets and early adoption of clean technologies.[30]

The idea of trading has broad support. For the IPCC, 'policies that provide a real or implicit price of carbon could create incentives for producers and consumers to significantly invest in local greenhouse gas products, technologies, and processes. Such policies could include economic instruments, government funding and regulation.'[31]

Evidence in support of trading

The EU scheme has tested the concept of emissions trading on an international scale. The results have been broadly positive. Participant companies have been encouraged to think strategically about their carbon emissions and reduce their production.[32] The UK also ran a domestic, voluntary trading environment for organisations wishing to gain early experience of trading, known as the 'UK Emissions Trading Scheme.' The scheme was successful in that participants reduced their emissions, despite weaknesses in the construction and operation of the scheme.[33]

28 Centre for Sustainable Energy, *A Rough Guide to Individual Carbon Trading: The ideas, the issues and the next steps* (November 2006)

29 David Fleming, *Energy and The Common Purpose: Descending the energy staircase with tradable energy quotas* (January 2007)

30 RSA Carbon*Limited*: *Exploring Personal Carbon Trading*, Briefing Paper (October 2006)

31 IPCC, *IPCC Fourth Assessment Report, Working Group III: Summary for Policymakers* (May 2007), Section E.23, p 28

32 DEFRA, *EU Emissions Trading Scheme – 2005 results for the UK: Summary Sheet 1 UK Summary* (September 2006)

33 DEFRA, *Appraisal of Years 1-4 of the UK Emissions Trading Scheme: A report by ENVIROS Consulting* (December 2006)

These two schemes are different in design. The EU scheme is based on a 'cap and trade' model that sets a limit for total CO_2 emissions from all the involved companies. Companies are then required to buy permits to cover their carbon production. The number of credits in the market is reduced over a period of time, raising the price of carbon. The scheme is designed to financially reward those companies that reduce their emissions the most and penalise those that do so by the least.

The UK scheme used a different model. In this scheme, a carbon baseline was set and money was made available to those participants able to reduce their carbon emissions below the baseline. Those who were successful received a financial reward, those that were not received nothing. Such an approach would not be cost neutral. Trading schemes demonstrate the potential of carbon trading between organisations. However, these schemes have not performed so well as to meet the climate change challenge alone. They fail to rise to the entirety of the climate change challenge in two key ways. Firstly, the scope is limited to large organisations that produce large amounts of carbon. Secondly, the scheme only covers a portion of total UK carbon emissions.

Personal carbon trading offers to overcome these two challenges. However, it has potential weaknesses. Firstly, such an approach would require everyone to participate in the scheme. Those with low levels of financial literacy might find it difficult to trade carbon permits. It might also punish those in the most precarious financial positions. Secondly, personal carbon trading may involve high transaction costs and be complicated and difficult to administer. There is as yet minimal data to support the introduction of such a scheme. While these issues do not necessarily rule-out a personal carbon trading scheme, they do mean that more work remains to be done.

Strengthening the local government role

It might be that local authorities have as yet unrealised potential to rise to the climate change challenge. To date, little research exists on the nature of the role local authorities might play. Neither does any evidence exist on the scale of reduction that local authorities might achieve. One of the reasons for this is that there are few incentives for councils to mitigate the effects of climate change. Local successes enjoyed by a small number of forward thinking councils result from the personal commitment of a small number of individuals.

This is despite the evolution of local government in recent years that has put councils in the position where they are capable of making a significant contribution to tackling climate change. The growing placeshaping role, as defined by Michael Lyons, asks individual authorities to combine their functions as, 'a place for discussion, representation and decision-making', with their role of, 'deliverer of the welfare state and public services.' These are to be married with, 'a desire to achieve efficient and responsive services and government.'[34] The combination of placeshaping with the more traditional service delivery and estate management roles offers councils a powerful portfolio of influence.

The effectiveness of this placeshaping role is dependent in large part on potential partners' perceptions of the capabilities of local government. To lead partnerships and wield influence councils need to be seen as worthy of the role. In recent years performance management has forced a rapid pace of improvement in local authorities. Exposure to external challenge has publicly exposed underperformance and helped to drive improvement. As the Local Government White Paper noted, 'A basket of Best Value Performance Indicators (BVPIs), designed to give a balanced picture of performance over time, shows councils have improved by 15.1 per cent between 2000/01 and 2004/05, and that the worst performers have improved faster than the rest.'[35]

The table on the right shows year-on-year increases in performance over the last four years.

Recent legislative reforms will also strengthen the package of powers that local government might use to address the climate change challenge. The impending Local Government and Public Involvement in Health Act will extend the influence of Local Area Agreements (LAAs); the main tool for pooling funding and priorities among local arms of the state. It will become mandatory for all local public bodies to co-operate in their operation and to negotiate with central government targets and indicators appropriate for their local areas.

Stronger LAAs will mean stronger Local Strategic Partnerships and a greater capacity for councils to build local coalitions among different parts of the state,

34 Sir Michael Lyons, *Place-shaping – a shared ambition for the future of local government* (March 2007), p 56

35 Local and Regional Governance Research Unit analysis, Communities and Local Government, 2006 from Department of Communities and Local Government, *Strong and Prosperous Communities: The Local Government White Paper* (October 2006), p 115, Section 6.8

Figure 2 Upper tier authorities – average annual performance by 2005 CPA category, indexed on 2001/02 results[36]

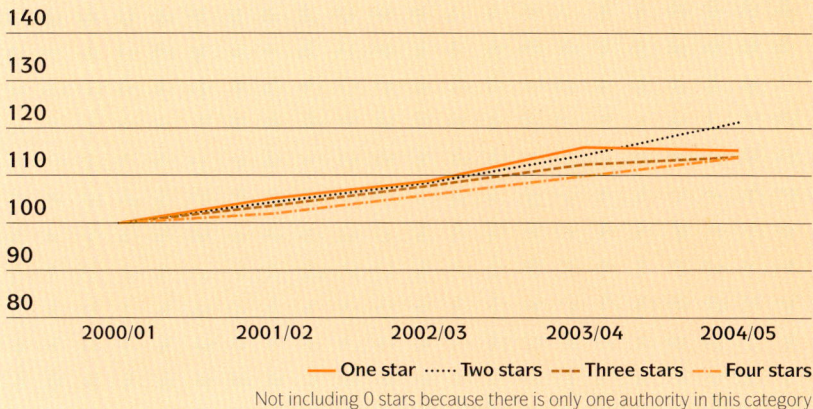

| | 2000/01 | 2001/02 | 2002/03 | 2003/04 | 2004/05 |

— One star ······ Two stars --- Three stars —·— Four stars

Not including 0 stars because there is only one authority in this category

and with private and third sector partners. The new Comprehensive Area Assessment performance regime, to be introduced in 2009, will look across local government, housing, health, education and community safety. It will further intertwine the priorities of local authorities with other local arms of the state.

Plans for this new performance regime reveal the Government's belief in the ability of local government to deliver. DEFRA recently consulted on a new set of climate change mitigation performance indicators for councils. These indicators will probably be divided into two main areas; firstly, reducing the production of CO_2 that results from a council's own activities and, secondly, reducing emissions that result from public services as well as from the wider community. This new facet to performance management might go some way to creating new incentives for local authorities to tackle climate change. But it is unlikely to drive the scale of change necessary to rise to the climate change challenge.

Little evidence exists on how far local authorities can drive change across the whole local authority area. Of the evidence that does exist, much focuses on the ability of local authorities to use their direct levers of control to reduce carbon

36 Department of Communities and Local Government, *Strong and Prosperous Communities: The Local Government White Paper* (October 2006), p 116 Section 6.9

emissions; either from their own estates or through reforming the operation of certain kinds of services.

The Carbon Trust is home to a wealth of information on practical actions that local authorities can take. Through their work on the Local Authority Carbon Management programme, the trust has developed a detailed understanding of how councils can manage their estates more effectively and reduce their environmental footprints. While this is essential work, it does not amount to a broad understanding of the role that local authorities can play in reducing emissions across the whole of the local area. Even if carbon emissions were reduced to zero, the carbon footprint of a whole area would remain close to present levels. For local authorities to make big cuts in greenhouse gas emissions across their local areas, it is necessary to look outside of those areas of direct control. Evidence from other areas suggests that the local government role might be more extensive.

For Lyons, local government can use its unique links with local people to tackle climate change. He summarises that, 'Addressing climate change and sustainable development will require individuals, as well as governments, to make different decisions…While people's 'environmental literacy' is increasing all the time, there is more to do to explain and influence behavioural change. Local government's closeness to the community should enable it to contribute to this as well, for example through work with schools and community groups.'[37]

The Local Government Association's (LGA) Climate Change Commission was, 'established to consider how local government can respond more effectively to both reduce greenhouse gas emissions and deal with the impact of climate change.' It is looking at local government's track record on tackling climate change, making recommendations to central and local government on improving the contribution of councils and raising awareness of how councils can tackle climate change with the Government and the public. The commission has asked consultants to conduct a literature review, to manage a survey of past local authority actions and to assess the impact of local authority actions.

The RSA is investigating the role of local authorities from a different perspective. A part of the Carbon Limited project is exploring the impact that personal carbon trading will have on those unwilling or unable to manage their own carbon

38 Sir Michael Lyons, *Lyons Inquiry into Local Government – Final Report* (March 2007), p70 Section 2.79

budgets. One idea is that local authorities can act as intermediaries; gathering data, assessing the capacity of local people to reduce their carbon footprints and giving advice.

NLGN research

This NLGN research project aims to plug these gaps in understanding. The project will gain a better understanding of the nature and extent of local government's offer to tackle climate change. It will also investigate how a new local authority trading scheme might create new incentives for councils to tackle climate change. In the process, it will uncover barriers to local government realising its potential and operating in a trading system. It will go on to make policy recommendations aimed at empowering the whole of the state to rise to the climate change challenge.

3 *Research design*

The research was designed to build a better understanding of local government's role in three areas: knowledge on the potential of local government, the offer of a trading environment and the barriers to both.

Interviews and case studies could have been used. But to develop this understanding an innovative design was more valuable. The research simulated a carbon trading system to gather data on how local government officers think their councils can tackle climate change. Experts gave their views on these suggestions. Research participants were drawn initially from eight local authorities across England.

The need for a better understanding of the potential of local government is clear. To gain this understanding, the research aimed to answer the following question:

- **To what extent are local authorities capable of addressing the climate change challenge by reducing greenhouse gas emissions across the local area?**

We hypothesised that local government could have a significant impact on carbon emissions across the whole of the locality. We also hypothesised that the unique attributes of local government might offer to make reductions more quickly than even central government aspirations. Solely focusing on those areas within the direct control of local authorities would not have a sufficient effect; even reducing all carbon emissions to zero from council buildings and fleets would not make a significant dent in the locality's footprint. Councils are only directly responsible for a small portion of local greenhouse gas emissions. But local authorities offer to affect wider behaviours by using their leadership role. Support for new trading solutions to provoke behavioural change is gaining ground.

At present, there are few incentives for local authorities to tackle climate change. It might be that an inter-authority carbon trading system would provide new cultural and financial pressure and incentives to reduce greenhouse gas emissions across the whole of the locality. It was reasonable to ask whether a trading system applied to local government might unlock its potential. The second question was therefore:

- **How far could an inter-local authority emissions trading scheme, where local authorities were asked to take responsibility for all local greenhouse gas emissions, create new drivers for local authorities to realise their potential?**

It is likely that placeshaping will offer the most potential for reducing greenhouse gas emissions. This placeshaping role is well-established and has been at the heart of thinking on local government reform for a number of years. The Local Government Act 2000 introduced new powers of well-being. These gave councils the freedom to do anything, within the legal framework, that would promote the economic, social or environmental well-being of local people. These new powers in theory opened the possibility for almost limitless local activity.

Despite these local well-being powers, the UK is failing to meet its self-imposed targets on reducing carbon emissions. This posed the question of how to create the environment within which local government would be persuaded to make the most of this potential. The third research question was therefore as follows:

- **What are the barriers to local government achieving its potential and to an inter-authority emissions trading environment?**

Once the terms of the research were defined, it was necessary to develop a research design that would answer these questions.

Research demands

The research could have used case studies to reveal the opinions of local environmental officers and other sustainability experts about the potential of local government. This would almost certainly have yielded interesting data on what individual councils were planning to do in the near future.

But the project was not aiming to understand solely what was happening in the next few years in a few selected council areas. Instead, we were aiming to develop an understanding of local government's capacity to deliver for years into the future. Also as there is little existing data on what can be achieved beyond actions in the direct control of councils, the data might have only revealed evidence on building management and sustainable procurement. Such evidence would have been unlikely to reveal the wider understanding of the potential of local authorities to make big reductions in carbon emissions necessary to meet the climate change challenge.

The potential of a carbon trading environment would also have been hard to judge through case studies. Only one local authority to date has direct experience of participating in a carbon trading system: Kirklees Council. Asking local authority officers exactly how they might deal with an unfamiliar, hypothetical future environment would have yielded limited results. The questions posed by this research project demand an understanding of the potential of local government stretching into the future. A different kind of design was therefore necessary.

Creating a simulation

Meeting this challenge required a design that could capture data on the potential of local government, assess the value of a carbon trading system and uncover potential barriers in both these areas. A design that used a market environment to stimulate ideas on ways of tackling climate change would generate data on both the potential of local government and the offer of a carbon trading system.

The solution was to design a research method that asked council environmental officers to operate in a hypothetical near-future scenario. In this environment, central government had charged local government with leading the fight against climate change. Local authorities would be required to buy carbon credits to cover greenhouse gas production across the whole local area. This would be conceptually similar to the EU Emissions Trading Scheme familiar to sustainability professionals.

The rules of the game

The simulation was to be electronic; conducted over email. It was to be played over five rounds. Each of the five rounds represented one virtual year. In each round, participants were asked to submit actions that would reduce the local area's carbon emissions for that year. Participants were asked to attach an estimated cost and estimated carbon saving to each action. Participants were also asked to consider the political viability of their suggestions. There was no limit to the number of actions taken in each round. A detailed timetable for the operation of the game is included in Appendix 2 of this report. A blank returns form is included in Appendix 3.

At the beginning of the simulation phase of the research process, each participating local authority was issued with a pack containing all the information necessary to participate in the simulation.

A sense of trading

The pack presented participants with a near-future scenario. In the scenario, consensus had been reached on the urgent need to tackle man-made climate change. The public was demanding a solution and businesses and the state were reacting.

The Climate Change Act had established a new national 'Carbon Committee' that was to oversee the transition to a low carbon economy. The Local Government Act 2007 has strengthened the role of councils as leaders of the whole of the local state. The second wave of Local Area Agreements and the new Comprehensive Area Assessment were changing the local environment. The idea of personal carbon trading as the solution to climate change was gaining popularity with sustainability experts and policymakers. Despite the potential of such a scheme, it was going to take time to develop and to win approval from the public.

Central government had given local government the task of dealing with climate change in the near future. The Government had placed a new legal duty on upper-tier local authorities to reduce carbon emissions across the whole area over the coming five years. Local authorities were to be required to match all carbon produced in the local area with carbon credits.

As a result, local authorities were presented with a whole new challenge. Local action would not be confined to reducing emissions from the local authority's estate. Instead, councils were asked to influence how individuals and organisations behave across the whole of the local area. No new powers were made available to councils bar those granted in the Local Government Act 2007.

Participants were told that they had been charged by the council's senior managers with leading the authority's approach. They were told that as the cost of credits rose they were responsible for making actions cost-effective. The scenario assured the participants that the Government would adequately resource the local authority to deliver on its new duties.

This research design sought to use a sense of trading to gather data on the future potential of local authorities and the effects of an inter-authority trading system; it was not intended to develop a technical model for an inter-authority greenhouse gas trading system. Rather, it applied conflicting price and demand pressures of a trading environment within the context of statutory targets.

Theoretical basis

This approach asked for an understanding of the working of domestic carbon trading systems. Yet no such system exists. A theoretical model that has gained attention is that developed by David Fleming in his work on Tradable Energy Quotas (TEQs).[38] In his model, individuals and organisations would be required to take responsibility for their environmental footprints by accounting for greenhouse gas emissions with government-issued permits purchased on a regulated market. Credit costs would fluctuate according to supply and demand.

In this system, the Government would create an independent Energy Policy Committee which would create a long-term carbon budget defining the rate of descent to a low carbon economy. The budget would set the number of carbon permits available in each year of personal carbon trading. These annual reductions would increase competition for credits, affecting price and creating growing financial incentives to reduce greenhouse gas emissions over time.

This model provided the basis for constructing the trading simulation at the centre of the research. NLGN could act as the Government, Energy Policy Committee and the market maker; issuing credits, setting the rate of descent and managing the market. Running a simulation over a period of years also provided the opportunity to give feedback on the measures to cut greenhouse gas emissions.

Finding the figures

Reliable data on the production of greenhouse gases by local authority area would be essential to make this research approach viable. Local authorities would need to have knowledge of the area's greenhouse gas production in order to make judgements on the volume of reductions necessary. Further, any claims made for amounts of CO_2 saved from a particular action would only be useful where they could be translated into a proportion of the area's production. Fortunately, DEFRA had recently published a set of figures that broke down CO_2 production by local authority area.[39]

---

38 David Fleming, *Energy and the Common Purpose: Descending the Energy Staircase with Tradable Energy Quotas, Second Edition* (January 2007)

39 Department for Environment, Food and Rural Affairs, *Experimental Statistics on Carbon Dioxide Emissions at Local Authority and Regional Level: 2004* (November 2006)

These figures are not perfect: their reliability in some areas is questionable; they are yet to be accepted as official government statistics; the methodology for collection has varied between years and as a result they are not comparable; and they only attempt to calculate carbon emissions rather than account for all greenhouse gas emissions. Methane, nitrous oxide and hydrofluorocarbons, for example, are not included. While CO_2 accounts for about 82 per cent of the UK's production of greenhouse gases, other gases have a greater warming potential.[40] The figures also exclude emissions from sources for which DEFRA judges that there was no clear basis for allocation to localities. As a result, domestic aviation, shipping and the offshore oil industry are excluded.

A combination of at least some of these weaknesses would undermine the statistics' usefulness in the real world, but not so for the research. They would be sufficient as long as the statistics were comparable between areas and would be accepted as sufficiently accurate by research subjects. Also, with the impending Climate Change Bill, the Government is focusing on setting targets for reducing CO_2 emissions rather than emissions of all greenhouse gases. CO_2 emissions have remained stubbornly high.

The figures also have a particular strength that would aid the research; they attribute CO_2 from energy usage to the end user rather than the producer; a classification that includes electricity generation and the rest of the energy production sector (for example refineries). All non-energy related emissions are attributed to the point of emission.

This approach draws a clear dividing line between businesses that provide electricity and fuel and those that do not. For example, CO_2 emissions from Drax, Europe's second biggest coal-fired power station, are not attributed to the Selby District Council or to North Yorkshire County Council. Instead, they would be attributed to electricity users. Emissions from all other kinds of industrial activity would be attributed to the areas in which they are produced. This model attributes those emissions from business that could be realistically affected by local action to each local area, while excluding emissions from businesses over which local authorities would be unlikely to have influence. Local responsibility cannot be expected to stretch to every aspect of public policy. The operation of the National Grid and large power stations feeding the Grid are likely to remain primarily a responsibility of central government.

---

[40] Department for Environment, Food and Rural Affairs, *UK Emissions of Air Pollutants 1970 to 2004* (December 2006), p 28

These figures were broken down to smallest possible local government unit. This means that allocations are made to districts rather than counties. Therefore, this means that figures for any counties that participated in the simulation would have to be simply calculated from their district emissions. As the simulation would seek the participation of only top-tier authorities, a county's emissions would be the sum total of its districts.

Setting the target

One of the hypotheses of this project is that local government might be capable of making rapid progress in reducing carbon emissions. The Government is about to set itself the legally binding target of reducing CO_2 emissions by a minimum of 26 per cent by 2020. If begun in 2008 and evenly distributed, this would translate into approximately 2.2 per cent annual reductions to 2020. Achieving this minimum goal would leave the remaining 34 per cent of reductions to be made over a period of 30 years, translating into approximately 1.1 per cent annual savings.

As described by Fleming, a carbon trading system would rely on a long-term target for reductions in greenhouse gas emissions. Trading would depend on this long-term target being broken into annual quotas of carbon permits. In this way, participants in the system would be able to develop annual plans for reducing emissions and for balancing the cost of credits with the cost of action.

A simulation would need to have a similar method for setting annual quotas. This need presented two questions; firstly, what should be the long-term reduction target? And secondly, over what period should the target be met? Both these questions had to be answered in such ways as to develop a workable simulation that was as close as possible to reality while not being over burdensome on the resources of research participants.

In March 2007, the European Commission made a commitment to reducing greenhouse gas emissions by 20 per cent of 1990 levels by 2020 across member states.[41] Current modelling suggests that the UK will come close to achieving this goal, with a 19 per cent reduction in emissions.[42] However, to construct a simulation to take place over this period of time would have placed

41 The Council of the European Union, *Presidency Conclusions, Brussels 8/9 March 2007* (2 May 2007), p12, Section 30

42 Cambridge Econometrics, UK Energy and the Environment Press Release: *The government's long-term targets for renewables and a low carbon future are at risk: CE forecasts provide a 'reality check' on the rhetoric of climate change* (27 August 2007)

an undue time burden on local authority participants. The Government's draft Climate Change Bill offered a different framework around which the simulation could be structured. The legislation will create new, legally-binding five year carbon budgets.

Five rounds of simulation would give the benefit of not overburdening local authorities while allowing the simulation to be extensive enough to capture meaningful data. The simulation would therefore take place over five virtual years and require a cut of 20 per cent in CO_2. Evenly distributed across the five years, this translates into four per cent annual reduction in CO_2 emissions. This tallies with the Mayor's Climate Change Action Plan, which commits the city to reducing carbon emissions by 60 per cent of 1990 levels by 2025. This asks for a four per cent annual cut. The simulation was designed to be challenging to participants and to require creativity. To set the bar too low might have allowed councils to concentrate on making reductions using only their tools of direct influence.

Pricing emissions

In a trading environment, the price of credits is a determining factor in creating incentives for reducing carbon emissions. A higher cost for credits would mean a higher cost for polluting, leading to a greater financial incentive to reduce greenhouse gas emissions. The EU-ETS has suffered from weak price incentives. Price peaked at around €30 per tonne of CO_2 in April 2006, but crashed to €10 per tonne by March 2007. As of September 2007, price had decreased further to €0.10, effectively ending trading for this iteration of the scheme.[43] Governments appear to have been too generous with carbon allowances. As a result, price incentives have disappeared.

Collapse of this kind was not a risk with the NLGN simulation. Price was only to appear to fluctuate with market demands, not to actually do so. Therefore, an unrealistic annual quota or major changes in the energy market would not undermine the simulation in the same way as the first phase of the EU-ETS.

In our simulation price ranges were arbitrarily fixed by NLGN allowing for some fluctuation year-on-year. The general price trend was to be upwards and these prices were not made public in advance. At the beginning of each round, an Analyst's Bulletin gave the forecast price for the following year, asserted with

43 Point Carbon Price Information, www.pointcarbon.com

varying degrees of certainty. Hypothetical events, such as major new entrants into the energy market, were introduced. Part of the reason was to introduce an element of uncertainty into the simulation. These events also justified the price changes experienced between years. The accuracy of these forecasts was revealed in the following year when it was explained whether the predicted events had occured and what the impact on price had been.

The Analyst's Bulletin also gave long-term predicted prices for credits, giving participants a level of certainty about what price would be at the end of the five-year simulation. This balanced the short-term uncertainty about price with an indication of price by the end of the simulation. This would allow for long-term planning for expenditure. Price was calculated using a simple graph.

The starting and finishing prices for carbon credits were decided according to the existing data on the price of carbon permits and the social cost of carbon. The starting price at the beginning of year one was £18 per tonne of CO_2. This was based on the period of peak prices experienced in the EU ETS in mid 2007 at the time of the project's construction. The finishing price at the end of year five was estimated to be £35-£40 per tonne. Stern accepts that his price of about £42 [44] is at the high end of estimations. Further details on the mechanism we used to decide prices are included in Appendix 5 of this report.

Action audit

Council officers have become used to receiving guidance on how to achieve their aims. Not to provide a frame of reference would have put officers in an unfamiliar position. The research was already asking officers to behave in unfamiliar ways and think as if in a hypothetical near future. The risk was that to present officers with too many unfamiliar challenges would undermine the quality and quantity of the data and detract from the central aims of the project.

To cater for this, the pack included a brief audit of areas in which local authorities had already taken action based on the three categories expressed in the Nottingham Declaration: 'estate manager and employer', 'service provider' and 'community leader'. Each category contained a brief description of the role of the local authority as well as four examples of past actions. We assumed that these three categories would be familiar to council environment officers familiar with the Nottingham Declaration.

---

[44] Based on 16 September 2007 exchange rates

Game participants

Willingness to be involved was the primary decider of which authorities would participate in the simulation. Eight local authorities originally agreed to be a part of the research, however councils that completed the simulation were:

- **Essex County Council**;

- **Havering London Borough Council**;

- **Lambeth London Borough Council**;

- **Lancashire County Council**;

- **Middlesbrough Council**;

- **Norfolk County Council**; and

- **Sheffield City Council**.

This group represented a wide range of different sorts of local authority from different parts of England; there were urban and rural areas, unitary authorities and counties, and differing levels of achievement in the most recent Comprehensive Performance Assessment. The involved authorities had differing levels of experience of reducing greenhouse gas emissions in their localities. Sheffield City, for example, has a longstanding climate change strategy. Others have a less well developed approach. This mix of experience was an important strength of the research as it allows for more reliable generalisations from the data.

Throughout the simulation, participants were to be referred to by anonymous designations. The above list does not tally with these designations. At the beginning of the research we decided to make submissions passed onto Expert Panel members anonymous. This approach was to ensure that local officers did not have to plan for the possibility that their ideas would become public. This might have led them to consider public reaction to their suggestions, meaning that they would be less ambitious than they otherwise would. Also, we intended to test the potential of local authorities in the future and not the present environment for taking action to tackle climate change, this reaction was to be avoided.

The Expert Panel

The packages of suggestions asked for as part of the simulation were to include officers' judgements for each action on financial costs, CO_2 savings and level of political favourability. These requests were built into the project for two reasons; firstly to encourage respondents to consider these three areas when formulating their returns and, secondly, to give the researcher powerful avenues for analysing the data.

The simulation relied on having figures available from which NLGN could calculate annual savings. However, to have directly translated figures provided by officers into CO_2 savings and costs would make a number of unrealistic assumptions that would have undermined the findings. Local officers have an informed view but there is a need for an objective assessment.

Therefore, at the end of each round, actions were anonymised and sent to an Expert Panel Member for assessment. The panel were asked to use their expertise to make assessments in the following two areas:

• **Would each action save the stated amount of carbon?**

• **Would each action cost the stated amount of money?**

To have assumed the absolute reliability of the attached judgements would have implied that respondents were equally accomplished as sustainability, finance and political experts. The professional positions of the research subjects would have made this level of expertise unlikely. Local authority environment officers are generally expert in the application of practical approaches to tackling climate change and compiling funding packages that can pay for action. Secondly, it would have assumed that local authority officers were well placed to understand the costs and savings that could be expected in the future. Even for the most accomplished expert, developing wholly reliable predictions of costs, savings and political favourability in a number of years time are unreasonable expectations.

This does not mean that the figures attached to each of the actions designed to tackle climate change were worthless. On the contrary, the project assumed that they would be vital in revealing the opinions of officers on the potential of different kinds of approaches to reduce CO_2 emissions.

The project would require the participation of experts in these two areas to make judgement on the quality packages of actions that could be translated into CO_2 savings for that year. Expertise that can be applied to the work of local authorities exists in academia, government agencies, local government and specific community organisations. We approached a number of people with reputations as experts in these areas to participate in the simulation. Those whom kindly agreed to participate were:

- **Dr Stewart Davies**, *Sustainable Development Commission, Commissioner for Business and Managing Director, Serco Integrated Services;*

- **Graeme Cameron**, *Assurance & Sustainability Manager, Serco;*

- **Philip Webber**, *Head of Environment, Kirklees Metropolitan Borough Council;*

- **Dr Christian Brand**, *Senior Researcher, Environmental Change Institute, Oxford University;*

- **Dr Tina Fawcett**, *Researcher, Environmental Change Institute, Oxford University;*

- **Ian Smith**, *Managing Director, Community Energy Plus;* and

- **Brooke Flanagan**, *Strategy Manager, Energy Savings Trust*.

Members of the Expert Panel were asked to make overall judgements on the quality of participants' full package of suggestions. The suggested actions were not to be scored individually. At the conclusion of each round of the simulation, anonymised forms were distributed to each member of the Expert Panel. There were two aspects to making an assessment. Firstly, experts were asked to make a judgement on the combined quality and viability of the suggestions. This judgement was to be translated into one of the scores in the below table:

Figure 3 Scores on expert judgements

	Expert score	NLGN carbon caving (% CO_2)
The suggestions are excellent	5	-8
The suggestions are very good	4	-6
The suggestions are good *This is a median score that would probably result in a 4 per cent carbon saving*	3	-4
The suggestions have shortcomings	2	-2
The suggestions are flawed	1	0

As the right column illustrates, these scores were to be translated into simple judgements on the amount of carbon saved resulting from the package.

Secondly, a box was provided for comments on aspects of the package. We suggested that comments might focus on the practicality of any suggestion, the numbers attached to each suggestion, and areas for improvement. Technical experts were asked to exclude from their scoring their opinions of the political viability of the packages of suggestions.

Assessing political viability asked for a different set of skills and was done separately and did not affect the CO_2 saving results. The political expert was asked:

- **How politically viable would each action be at the local level?**

Political judgements would be less time consuming to make than scoring the technical viability of packages of suggestions. Chris Leslie, former government minister, former councillor and Director of NLGN provided a brief assessment of the viability of the suggestions based on his experience.

Using the Expert Panel in this way generated scores for participant local authorities that could be translated into carbon savings. It also created a rich feedback loop that would help to improve the progress of the research participants over the course of the simulation.

Feedback mechanisms

As mentioned previously, the Expert Panel was employed in part to generate feedback for the participants. This feedback was given by email after each round of the simulation in order to inform suggestions made in the next. This feedback, given by email, was designed to have five elements:

- **estimated carbon saving**;

- **estimated value of carbon saving (£)**;

- **equivalent cost of credits to cover the carbon amount saved (£)**;

- **summarised technical comments from Expert Panel members**; and

- **summarised political comments from Political Expert**.

Structuring the feedback in this way was intended to help local authority participants improve their approaches year-on-year. The most important aspect of the feedback would be the information on cost of actions to save CO_2 and the equivalent cost of credits had that amount of CO_2 not been saved. This information was provided to encourage thinking about cost-effectiveness rather than absolute cost of producing CO_2 emissions. An example of a feedback email can be found in Appendix 3 of this document.

Feedback of this kind was planned for rounds one to four. However, it would not have been appropriate to give this feedback after round five; there would be no next round to inform. Instead, a meeting was planned to follow the final round of the simulation to be attended by as many of the participants in the simulation and members of the expert panel as possible. This meeting had two main purposes. The first was to give participants and expert panel members feedback on both the results of round five and progress over the whole period of the game. The second was to gather more data on the experience of the simulation, to discuss some of the early findings and to explore approaches to empowering local authorities.

Mid-simulation feedback on progress against target and cost-effectiveness would take place at the end of round three. This was to give participants the chance to see the progress that the whole group had made towards reducing carbon emissions by four per cent each year. It was also to reinforce the idea of cost-effectiveness.

Drivers of performance

One of the purposes of this design was to give local officers three incentives to construct the most effective possible approaches to reducing CO_2 emissions across their locality. The research was designed to push officers as far as was practical. The first driver was the creation of targets. The councils were each given four per cent annual reduction targets, totalling 20 per cent over the course of the simulation. This gave officers a benchmark against which they could measure their own performance. It also created a measure that could be used to assess the quality of each individual measure.

The second incentive was competition. The simulation generated statistics on the performance of each council. This could allow us to make comparisons between the levels of success achieved in each local authority, leading to rankings. Despite guaranteeing that we would not identify which councils had achieved which savings, the participants were free to identify themselves. This encouraged local authorities to compete to be the best at reducing CO_2.

The third incentive was financial. The annual feedback gave participants detail on how much CO_2 they saved in the previous year. It also told participants the cost of the credits that would have been neccessary had no action been taken. This created the opportunity for officers to suggest actions that not only saved CO_2 but also saved the council money.

Shape of the simulation

The below diagram summarises the shape of the research:

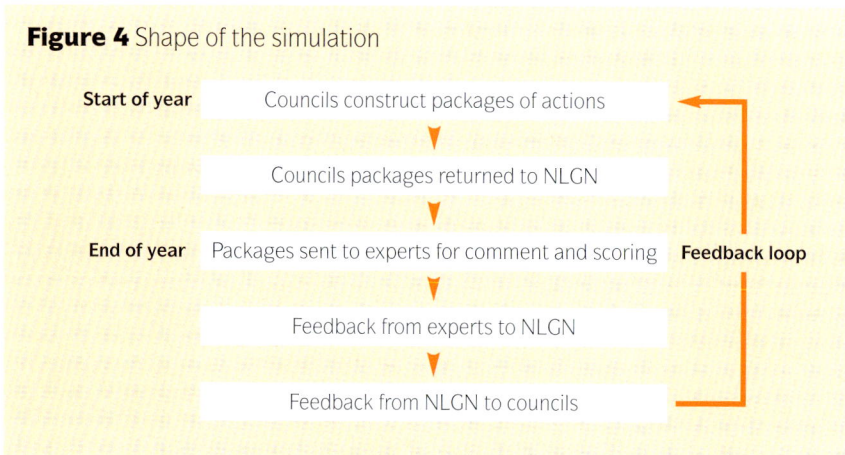

Figure 4 Shape of the simulation

Start of year	Councils construct packages of actions
	Councils packages returned to NLGN
End of year	Packages sent to experts for comment and scoring — **Feedback loop**
	Feedback from experts to NLGN
	Feedback from NLGN to councils

4 *Results and findings*

Pursuing the target

All local authorities made significant savings. The performance of the councils varied; some achieved higher savings than others. Results across all the local authorities demonstrate a significant level of potential. Even the least successful local authority managed to make significant savings. There is a general trend of improvement over time as the simulation progressed. Operating in the simulation affected the way that local officers behaved.

This section examines the role of the expert panel members and their judgements on each local authority's progress towards the target.[45] It goes on to look at performance across the whole of the market and what this tells us about the potential of local government to tackle climate change. It then compares this potential to existing plans for reducing carbon emissions. It goes on to draw conclusions about the potential of local government to tackle climate change and the pace of the progress that can be made towards a low carbon economy.

Experts and scoring

The simulation relied on the expertise of a number of experienced sustainability professionals. The experts were not asked to make detailed, quantitative assessments of the packages presented to them. This would have been too time-consuming and, for some, outside the scope of their professional experience. Their role was to examine the packages of actions submitted each year and make a judgement on the accuracy of the figures attached to each of the suggestions. Experts gave an overall score to the package, but not to the individual actions within each package. This score was an expression of their judgement on how much CO_2 the package would save. We then converted this score into an annual saving. Experts were also asked to comment on the packages and make suggestions for improvement.

The scoring was helpful in two ways. Firstly, it gave us a simple method of judging savings in each year. Secondly, it removed the risk of relying on unrealistic figures.

---

[45] The simulation concluded after three and a half weeks with seven of the original eight local authorities completing the simulation. One local authority was compelled to drop-out of the simulation before the start of round one. This left us with seven sets of results with which to work.

The research could not assume that officers would have the information available to generate wholly realistic figures for each action over five rounds for up to six years in the future. A second opinion adds greater validity and reliability to the research. We used these scores to calculate annual savings for each authority for each year. The following section summarises the scoring for each local authority.

Local authority one

This local authority was the least successful in making CO_2 reductions when looked at as a proportion of the 2004 baseline. Even so, despite not meeting the

Figure 5 Local authority one – progress against target

Target (% of 2004 CO_2 baseline)	Expert panel reduction score (% of 2004 CO_2 baseline)	End-year target (ktonnes 2004 CO_2 baseline)	End-year CO_2 (ktonnes)	CO_2 saving (ktonnes)
1	0	1,472	1,533	0
2	2	1,410	1,502	30.7
3	2	1,349	1,471	30.7
4	4	1,288	1,410	61.3
5	n/a[46]	1,226	1,410	n/a

1600 CO_2 ktonnes
1550
1500
1450
1400
1350
1300
1250
1200

Year 1   Year 2   Year 3   Year 4   Year 5

— Cumulative end-year target (ktonnes CO_2 2004 baseline)
— Actual whole end-year target (ktonnes CO_2 2004 baseline)

46 No return was made in year five

20 per cent target set by the simulation, the council made significant progress in reducing emissions. Overall, the saving was approximately 122.7 kilotonnes, representing a reduction of about eight per cent of the baseline. This is equivalent to the amount of CO_2 produced by 3,408 average UK homes over five years.[47] This is despite not submitting a return in year five. If this return had been submitted and the trend of savings had been sustained we can assume that a further four per cent would have been saved in the final year. This would have seen an overall reduction of around 184 tonnes, or a 12 per cent reduction. So, although significant reductions were made, the final outcome was well short of the 20 per cent target.

Over the four years for which the council made submissions, expert panel members judged that the packages of suggestions were saving the same as or more than the previous year. Savings in year four, the final year for which a submission was made, were greater than savings made in years one, two and three. As the graph demonstrates, there was improvement over time. This suggests that aspects of the simulation were responsible for this improvement.

Comments made during the simulation give an indication of its effects. The responsible officer noted that, in year one, the expert panel member judged the amount of CO_2 saved as zero. This was despite the fact that the package of actions relied on approaches previously tested in other local authority areas under the guidance of external sustainability experts. The problem with the package was not its technical correctness but its scale; the amount saved was only a tiny fraction of the four per cent target, meaning that savings were closer to zero than to two per cent. This gave it a zero score. This experience appeared to spur the officer to do better. From this point forward, for the three subsequent years for which returns were made, expert panel members awarded savings.

Local authority two

The council made significant progress in reducing emissions compared to its 2004 CO_2 baseline. It was one of three to surpass its 20 per cent target by

---

[47] Based on figures from DEFRA and the Barker Review of Land Use Planning. There was an estimated 538,315 kilotonnes of CO_2 produced in the UK, not including domestic aviation, offshore gas & oil and shipping, in 2004. There are 24m homes in the UK which account for 27 per cent of CO_2 emissions. The average UK home therefore produces 6.06 tonnes of CO_2 annually, meaning 0.036 kilotonnes over five years

Figure 6 Local authority two – progress against target

Target (% of 2004 CO$_2$ baseline)	Expert panel reduction score (% of 2004 CO$_2$ baseline)	End-year target (ktonnes 2004 CO$_2$ baseline)	End-year CO$_2$ (ktonnes)	CO$_2$ saving (ktonnes)
1	0	9,724	10129.00	0
2	4	9,319	9723.84	405.16
3	8	8,914	8913.52	810.32
4	4	8,508	8508.36	405.16
5	6	8,103	7900.62	607.74

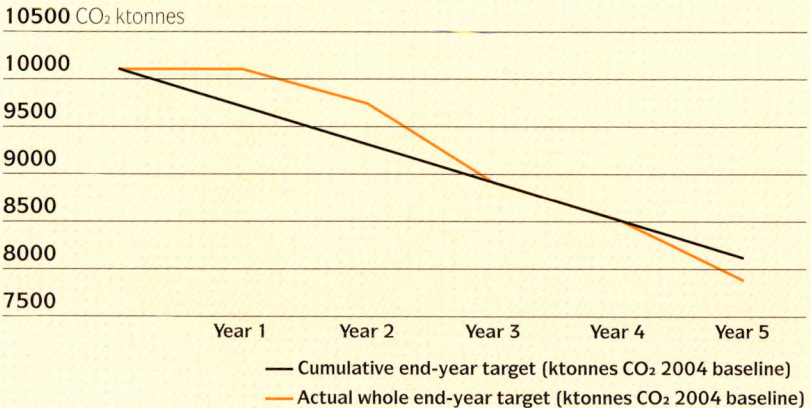

—— Cumulative end-year target (ktonnes CO$_2$ 2004 baseline)
—— Actual whole end-year target (ktonnes CO$_2$ 2004 baseline)

saving 22 per cent. This translates into a saving of 2,228.38 kilotonnes over the five years. This is equivalent to the amount of CO$_2$ produced by 61,899 average UK homes in five years.[48] This is an overall reduction of 22 per cent on the simulation baseline. This council therefore exceeded the 20 per cent target and was one of the three to do so. Returns were submitted for every round of the simulation.

Again, performance showed improvement over time. In the first year, despite making a submission, the expert panel awarded savings of zero. In every subsequent year, the council met or exceeded the four per cent target. This improvement in performance saw the council make-up for the zero savings in the first year and eventually exceed that 20 per cent target.

48 See footnote 43

Comments from the submitting officer during the simulation suggested that the experience of trading was again encouraging improvement. In the early rounds, the officer chose to focus on approaches already in development. By the later rounds, the officer felt that these pre-existing approaches had been exhausted, forcing a move to more ambitious initiatives. The early rounds of the simulation were an exercise in projecting existing thinking into the future. By the final two rounds, the officer felt it necessary to take a 'blue skies' approach and produce more ambitious actions.

Local authority three

The council made significant progress in reducing carbon emissions when compared to its 2004 baseline. The responsible officer made returns for each round and was one of the three authorities to exceed its 20 per cent target, saving a total of 25 per cent by the end of year five. This translates into a saving of about 1,910.75 kilotonnes CO_2, equivalent to the amount produced by

Figure 7 Local authority three – progress against target

Target (% of 2004 CO_2 baseline)	Expert panel reduction score (% of 2004 CO_2 baseline)	End-year target (ktonnes 2004 CO_2 baseline)	End-year CO_2 (ktonnes)	CO_2 saving (ktonnes)
1	4	7,337	7337.28	305.72
2	6	7,032	6878.70	458.58
3	2	6,726	6725.84	152.86
4	5	6,420	6343.69	382.15
5	8	6,114	5732.25	611.44

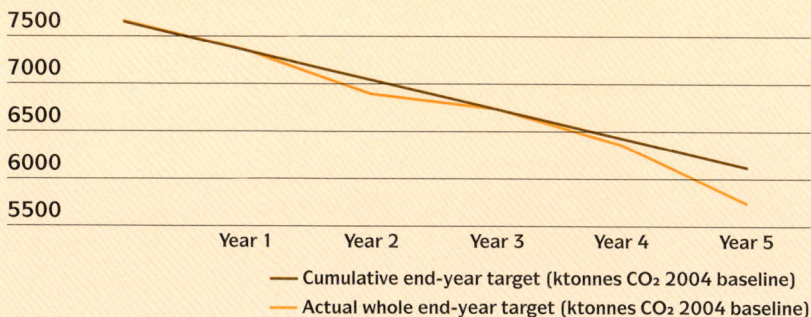

8000 CO_2 ktonnes

7500

7000

6500

6000

5500

Year 1   Year 2   Year 3   Year 4   Year 5

—— Cumulative end-year target (ktonnes CO_2 2004 baseline)
—— Actual whole end-year target (ktonnes CO_2 2004 baseline)

53,076 average UK homes over five years.[49] Returns were made in every one of the five rounds.

Evidence of improvement over time is less prominent in this set of results. The fact that at no point did the authority miss its four per cent target could be a factor; improvement on the previous year was not necessary to achieve the minimum standard. The lowest annual savings came in year three with just a two per cent saving. The highest annual saving came in round five. At no point did this council drop below the annual four percent reduction target despite the poor result in year two.

The comments of the participating officer made during the final feedback session suggested that as the simulation progressed he was encouraged to think differently about his role. At the beginning of the simulation, he considered how to combine pots of public funding. By the end, he was considering how to raise finance by suggesting actions that would generate their own revenue. Making the connection between environmental objectives and financial considerations was vital in allowing him to make realistic suggestions that would be within the financial constraints laid-out in the scenario.

Local authority four

This council originally agreed to be a part of the research although was unable to participate in the simulation.

Local authority five

This authority also made large savings on its 2004 baseline although was not one of the authorities that managed to exceed its 20 per cent target. The council made a 12 per cent saving by the end of year five which translates into savings of about 1,315.56 kilotonnes of CO_2. This is roughly equivalent to the output of 36,543 average UK homes over the same period.[50] No return was made during year two.

This set of results clearly shows an acceleration in performance over time. In the first year, no savings were awarded by the Expert Panel. In the second year no return was made, resulting in zero savings. By the beginning of round three the responsibility had been passed to a colleague. At this point, performance began to improve with a steady ascent in savings. The last three rounds of the simulation show an average annual saving of four per cent. Also, every one of the last three years realised a greater saving than the previous year.

---

49 and 50 See footnote 43

Figure 8 Local authority five – progress against target

Target (% of 2004 CO₂ baseline)	Expert panel reduction score (% of 2004 CO₂ baseline)	End-year target (ktonnes 2004 CO₂ baseline)	End-year CO₂ (ktonnes)	CO₂ saving (ktonnes)
1	0	10,524	10963.00	0
2	n/a[51]	10,086	10963.00	0
3	2	9,647	10743.74	219.26
4	4	9,209	10305.22	438.52
5	6	8,770	9647.44	657.78

11500 CO₂ ktonnes
11000
10500
10000
9500
9000
8500
8000

Year 1   Year 2   Year 3   Year 4   Year 5

—— Cumulative end-year target (ktonnes CO₂ 2004 baseline)
—— Actual whole end-year target (ktonnes CO₂ 2004 baseline)

These results suggest that the council took some time to get used to operating in the simulation. A change in the responsible officer at end of round two meant that there was no return for that round. The office that took over the simulation was able to commit the required time. The result was a sustained improvement in the performance of the authority.

Local authority six

This authority also made large savings on its 2004 baseline but did not manage to reach its 20 per cent target. The council made 12 per cent savings by the end of year five, which translates into a CO₂ saving of 552.0 kilotonnes. This is equivalent

---

51 No return was made in year two

to the amount of CO_2 produced by 15,333 average UK homes over the same period.[52] Returns were made in every round of the simulation.

This set of results shows some improvement over time. A saving of four per cent was made in year four, compared to savings of two per cent in other years. This council therefore did not sustain improvement in performance. Only between years three and four was there an acceleration in savings. Thereafter, the level of saving returned to that of the previous three years.

Comments by the responsible officer at the feedback meeting reveal that the simulation applied pressure to improve. He was keen to compete with his peers and be successful in the simulation. However, he did not feel that he had the same potential as other local authorities to improve as so much progress had

Figure 9 Local authority six – progress against target

Target (% of 2004 CO_2 baseline)	Expert panel reduction score (% of 2004 CO_2 baseline)	End-year target (ktonnes 2004 CO_2 baseline)	End-year CO_2 (ktonnes)	CO_2 saving (ktonnes)
1	2	4,416	4508.00	92.00
2	2	4,232	4416.00	92.00
3	2	4,048	4324.00	92.00
4	4	3,864	4140.00	184.00
5	2	3,680	4048.00	92.00

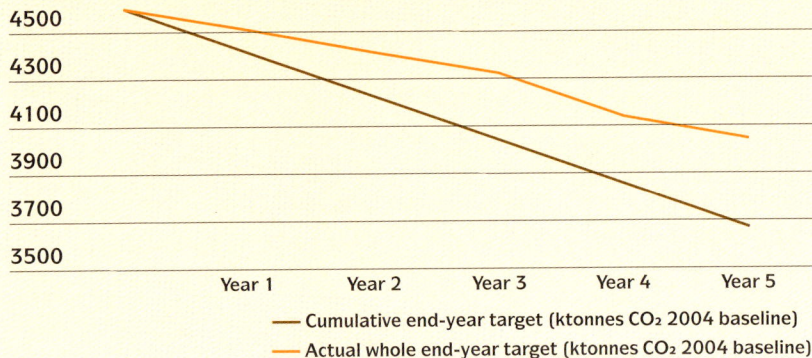

— Cumulative end-year target (ktonnes CO_2 2004 baseline)
— Actual whole end-year target (ktonnes CO_2 2004 baseline)

52 and 53 See footnote 43

previously been made in his council. He would have valued information on the progress of other participating councils.

Local authority seven

This authority made the largest saving when compared with its 2004 baseline and was one of the three to meet or exceed the 20 per cent target. It made a 28 per cent saving, which translates into 398.72 kilotonnes of CO_2. This is equivalent to the CO_2 produced by 11,076 average UK homes.[53] Returns were made for every round of the simulation.

Figure 10 Local authority seven – progress against target

Target (% of 2004 CO_2 baseline)	Expert panel reduction score (% of 2004 CO_2 baseline)	End-year target (ktonnes 2004 CO_2 baseline)	End-year CO_2 (ktonnes)	CO_2 saving (ktonnes)
1	4	1,367	1367.04	56.96
2	4	1,310	1310.08	56.96
3	8	1,253	1196.16	113.92
4	6	1,196	1110.72	85.44
5	6	1,139	1025.28	85.44

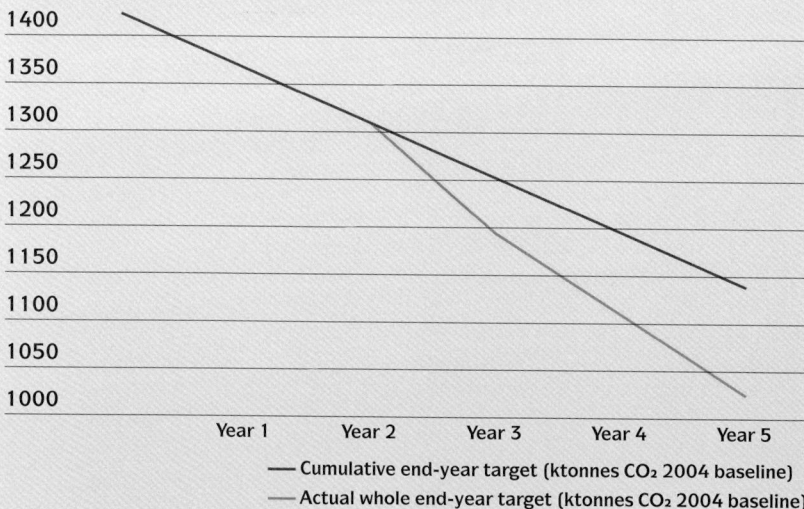

1450 CO_2 ktonnes
1400
1350
1300
1250
1200
1150
1100
1050
1000

Year 1   Year 2   Year 3   Year 4   Year 5

—— Cumulative end-year target (ktonnes CO_2 2004 baseline)
—— Actual whole end-year target (ktonnes CO_2 2004 baseline)

These results show some improving performance between years. This is despite the authority never feeling the pressure of missing a yearly target. As a result, at no point did this council fall behind the five year target. The most effective package of suggestions was made in year three where savings of eight per cent were made.

Comments from the responsible officer at the feedback event suggest that the simulation helped to drive her to improve. At the feedback event, the responsible officer indicated her delight at reducing CO_2 by the largest proportion. The element of competition in the simulation had motivated her to achieve large CO_2 savings.

Local authority eight

In common with other participants, this authority made substantial reductions in CO_2 emissions when compared to its 2004 baseline. It did not however reach the

Figure 11 Local authority eight – progress against target

Target (% of 2004 CO_2 baseline)	Expert panel reduction score (% of 2004 CO_2 baseline)	End-year target (ktonnes 2004 CO_2 baseline)	End-year CO_2 (ktonnes)	CO_2 saving (ktonnes)
1	4	1,101	1101.12	45.88
2	2	1,055	1078.18	22.94
3	2	1,009	1055.24	22.94
4	0	963	1055.24	0.00
5	4	918	1009.36	45.88

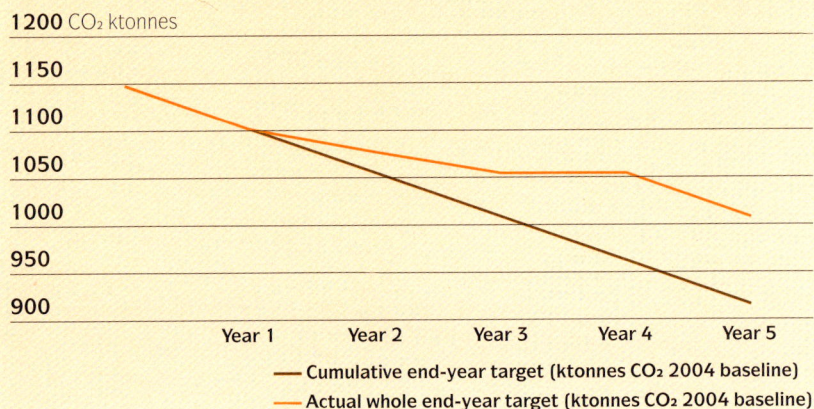

Cumulative end-year target (ktonnes CO_2 2004 baseline)
Actual whole end-year target (ktonnes CO_2 2004 baseline)

20 per cent reduction target. It managed to achieve reductions of 12 per cent over the course of the whole simulation, which translates into savings of about 137.64 kilotonnes of CO_2. This is equivalent to the amount produced by 3,823 average UK homes over five years.[54] Returns were made for every round of the simulation.

These results do not demonstrate improvement in performance between years as clearly as results from other authorities. The four per cent savings made in the first year are equal to those made in the final year. The worst performing year was year four, after progress being made towards the target in the first three years. The improvement between years four and five suggest that being given a zero score in year four might have promoted improvement in year five.

Comments by the responsible officer suggest that this was the case. After receiving the poor score in year four, the responsible officer contacted NLGN to discuss the reasons for the poor score and how to improve her approach in the following year. Without the feedback loop it was unlikely that performance would have been improved to the extent it was.

Whole market progress

The average performance of all seven local authorities will reveal the potential of local government. This performance can be measured by the cumulative amount of CO_2 saved every year across the whole market. The extent to which the targets were met will show how far councils have the potential to rise to the climate change challenge.

The simulation gave participants challenging annual CO_2 reduction targets. These targets created a benchmark against which participants could test their rates of progress and hence incentives to reduce CO_2 emissions as far as possible. Figure 12 overleaf summarises the results across all seven local authorities over the five years of the simulation.

Group performance

As can be seen from Figure 12 overleaf, the whole group of local authorities did not reach its 20 per cent target by the end of year five. However, the group did achieve a saving of 17.8 per cent on the 2004 baseline at an average annual saving of 3.56 per cent. This translates into a saving of 6,665.69 kilotonnes of

---

54 See footnote 43

Figure 12 Summary of all simulation results over the five year period

Cumulative target (% of 2004 CO2 baseline)	Cumulative end-year target (ktonnes 2004 CO2 baseline)	Actual whole end-year progress (ktonnes 2004 CO2 baseline)	End-year baseline (ktonnes CO2)	Annual reduction (% of 2004 CO2 baseline)	Increase in % saved over previous year	Cumulative reduction (% of 2004 CO2 baseline)
4	35,941	500.56	36,938.44	1.34	n/a	1.34
8	34,444	1,066.30	35,872.14	2.85	1.51	4.19
12	32,946	1,441.96	34,430.18	3.85	1.0	8.04
16	31,449	1,556.59	32,873.59	4.16	0.31	12.19
20	29,951	2,100.28	30,773.31	5.61	1.45	17.80
TOTAL		6,665.69				

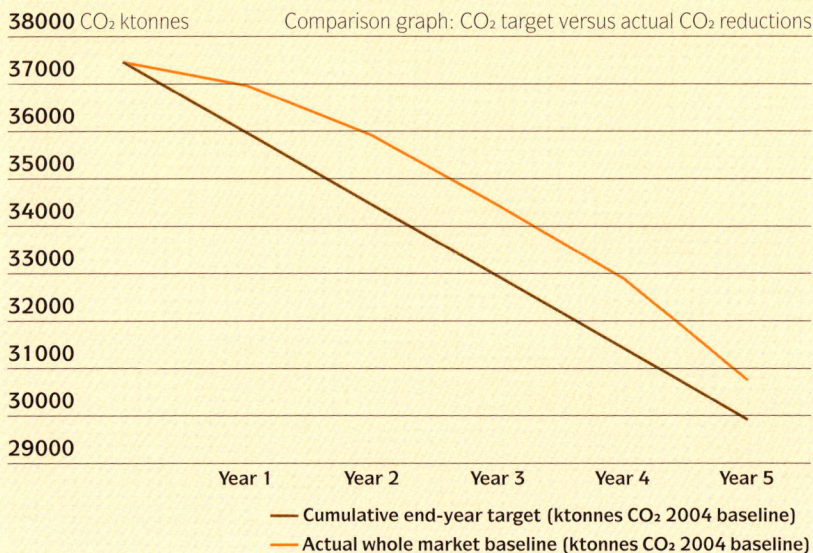

38000 CO2 ktonnes — Comparison graph: CO2 target versus actual CO2 reductions

— Cumulative end-year target (ktonnes CO2 2004 baseline)
— Actual whole market baseline (ktonnes CO2 2004 baseline)

CO2, equivalent to the amount produced by approximately 185,158 average UK homes over five years.[55]

But only seven councils participated in the simulation, with a total CO2 footprint of only 6.95 per cent of total UK emissions. It is useful to illustrate what the

55 See footnote 43

effects of these kinds of savings would be if mirrored across the whole of the UK. If the same 17.8 per cent reduction was achieved by all councils, the saving would be 95,820.07 kilotonnes over five years, equivalent to 2,661,669 average UK homes over the same period.[56] Or, in other words, the equivalent of completely removing from the atmosphere all the CO_2 produced by 11 per cent of the UK's housing by the end of the fifth year.

It is also revealing to speculate on the scale of savings that would be realised if the performance of the most successful local authority, LA7, was projected across the whole of the UK. This council managed to reduce CO_2 production by a total of 28 per cent from the 2004 baseline over the five years of the simulation. Projected across the UK, savings would be 150,728.20 kilotonnes of CO_2. This is equivalent to the amount produced by 4,186,894 average UK homes in five years. Or, the equivalent of completely removing the amount of CO_2 produced by 17 per cent of the UK's homes over five years.

These statistics are striking. Local authorities clearly offer a huge amount of potential for reducing CO_2 emissions across their local areas. They are all the more striking for reflecting the opinions of independent sustainability experts. Without this filter, it might be said that local officers were misjudging the potential of their councils. But with the filter both the validity and the reliability of the findings are reinforced.

Ranking performance

Figure 13 overleaf ranks the local authorities according to the proportion of CO_2 they were able to save on their 2004 baselines.

This comparison shows large differences in the proportion of the baseline saved by each local authority. Despite these variations, even the least successful local authority was able to make significant reductions. The rankings show no correlation between size of CO_2 baseline and performance. Neither can success be explained by differences in the research model; all participants were required to operate in exactly the same scenario. Also, there appears to be no correlation between location, structure, or Comprehensive Performance Assessment (CPA) score.[57]

---

56 See footnote 43
57 Details of location, structure, political control and CPA score would reveal the identities of the local authorities and for this reason they are omitted

Figure 13 Ranking performance

LA4 is not included – see footnote 45

Local authority	Rank	Total reduction (% CO_2)	annual reduction (% CO_2)	Average Actual saving (ktonnes CO_2)
LA7	1	28%	5.6%	399
LA3	2	25%	5.0%	1,911
LA2	3	22%	4.4%	2,228
LA5	4	12%	2.4%	1,316
LA6	5	12%	2.4%	552
LA8	6	12%	2.4%	138
LA1	7	8%	1.6%	123

The feedback meeting at the end of the simulation found that local circumstances were the most influential determinants of success. It is reasonable to attribute the variations in performance to specific local circumstances. Evidence from the final feedback meeting at the end of the simulation supports this. LA7 revealed that the actions suggested during the simulation were under development in the real world. The officer had adapted many of these actions to the simulation; the council is currently consulting on its detailed and ambitious climate change strategy. Other authorities that performed well revealed that they were undergoing similar processes.

This suggests that success is dependent on forethought and detailed planning. It is reasonable to assume that if all the local authorities were to engage in the same planning process, they could achieve similar success. This suggests that with additional help and guidance the achievements of the least successful might be raised to the level of the most. Participants were also in broad agreement that councils have a lot of potential to reduce CO_2 emissions. But, there are numerous practical barriers to realising this potential. Removing these barriers, both national and local, is a key aspect of realising the potential of local government.

At present, the environment within which councils operate does not provide the incentives necessary to push climate change towards the top of the agenda. There was some agreement from local officers that a four per cent target was achievable if barriers to local action were removed. All participants were in agreement that the current top-down performance management regime does not reward local authorities for success in reducing CO_2 emissions.

On the contrary, the present system imposes indirect penalties for those authorities that divert too many resources from the core business of delivering on the needs of local people and the performance management targets of central government. The current system is an active hindrance. Further, councils themselves are not well equipped to tackle this important issue: the necessary data is lacking, the priorities of different departments are not always aligned and the interaction between financial considerations and environmental objectives are not as prevalent as necessary. If these barriers can be overcome then four per cent annual CO_2 savings are realistic.

Conclusions

Local authorities have huge potential to reduce CO_2 emissions across their local areas; if average savings made during the simulation were repeated across the UK, just under 96,000 kilotonnes of CO_2 would be saved over five years. If the performance of the most successful authority was repeated across the UK then 151,000 kilotonnes could be saved. The later figure is equivalent to the amount of CO_2 produced by over four million average UK homes over five years. Even the local authority that made the least savings made significant reductions. This potential is as yet largely unexploited.

Those authorities that were planning real-world approaches to tackling climate change were the most successful. Four per cent annual reductions are realistic if barriers to action are removed. At present, both barriers in the national and local environment exist. These need to be overcome before the potential can be realised.

Improvement over time

The simulation was designed to examine how far an inter-authority trading scheme might help to realise local government's potential to tackle climate change. To uncover this, it is necessary to examine the extent to which performance varied over the five years. If it is the case that improvement was better as time went on, there is a case to say that some aspects of the trading simulation were responsible.

As Figure 12 in the previous section shows, average performance across the whole market improved over time. In every year, the amount of carbon saved was greater than the previous year. This is particularly striking in years four and five where the whole market surpassed its four per cent annual target, achieving savings of 4.16 per cent and 5.61 per cent respectively. If the whole of the UK were to reach the performance seen in year five then a total of 30,199.47 kilotonnes of CO_2 annually. This is equivalent to the CO_2 produced by 4,194,371 average UK homes in one year.

As familiarity with the trading environment grew, so did the performance of the local authorities. This might have been the result of an increasing understanding of the simulation. It could also be due to the effect of the constructive feedback from experts that was fed back to the participant councils at the beginning of each year. A competitive spirit could also be a factor; as the simulation progressed, the desire to achieve more than other participants appeared to grow.

Comments at the final feedback meeting reinforce these findings. An expert panel member noted that the suggestions appeared to improve from year three onwards. Even though this expert, as with all panel members, only saw a random selection of the packages of suggestions in any one year it is still revealing. Several participants agreed that the luxury of time to consider actions to reduce CO_2 emissions allowed them to improve their approaches over time. This was felt to be at least as valuable as the expert feedback and sense of trading. A barrier to this in the real world would be finding enough staff time to allocate to the construction and execution of plans to reduce CO_2 emissions.

The feedback meeting also revealed that the element of competition between councils helped to drive improving performance between years. All participants wanted to demonstrate that they were capable of saving the largest proportions of their baseline when compared to other authorities. Those authorities that had performed less well were keen to understand the approaches of other councils. Those that were most successful were keen to highlight their success and share their approaches. This is despite the fact that during the simulation one council was not aware of the performance of the others.

The rate of improvement

Another revealing aspect of performance over time can be seen in the differences in the amounts saved each year. The results here are less clear than simple improvement in performance; performance did not necessarily accelerate year-on-year, despite the sustained growth in CO_2 savings. The rate of improvement as measured by increases in the percentage savings over the previous year fluctuated markedly. In year two, the group managed to save an extra 1.51 per cent when compared to the previous year. In year three, the extra saving was 1.0 per cent. In year four, the additional saving was down to an extra 0.31 per cent when compared to the previous year. In year five, the increase was back up to near the year two level, with an increase of 1.45 per cent on the previous year.

In part, this fluctuation in the rate of improvement reflects the complex nature of the task allocated to the local authorities. The feedback meeting revealed the extent to which the idea of trading, the need to make annual CO_2 reduction, the inability to exchange good practice between councils and the requirement to think in a different way about finance put officers in unfamiliar positions.

However, it is reasonable to explore the idea that this fluctuation was not simply the result of uncertainty. The data shows two similar periods of rapid acceleration; between years one and two and years four and five as well as two periods of lesser acceleration, between years two and three and years three and four. By year two, after the first round of expert feedback, it is likely that officers were more comfortable with the simulation. The unfamiliarity of the environment had been overcome.

In year two officers could submit actions already in the planning stages. By the third year, however, these pre-planned actions were becoming less readily available and the rate of improvement again slowed. By the fourth year, the task was becoming more difficult as planned actions had already been submitted. However, there is a large upturn in performance in year five. This can be explained in two ways. Firstly as increase in ambition as the task became harder. Officers were challenged to save more and they rose to the challenge. The mid-simulation feedback, which gave progress against targets for the whole of the market, might have encouraged this greater ambition. Secondly, the simulation was drawing to an end. Officers could see how well they were delivering on their targets and to what extent they would have to raise their games to deliver 20 per cent reductions. The amount they had to save in the final year was obvious.

Evidence from the feedback meeting supports these assumptions. Officers took some time to get used to operating in an unfamiliar environment. Once they were familiar with the challenge they were able to better deliver on its demands. Space to think was important in driving improvement, as mentioned previously.

For one officer in particular, taking part in the simulation revealed that the council's existing plans were too conservative.

The trading element of the simulation also forced creativity. In part, this was to do with competition; not to find savings would risk performing less well than peers in other authorities. Its demands meant that officers had to find new ways of delivering savings. Participants were encouraged to move away from assumptions about cost and think more creatively. Those councils most successful at reducing emissions were those that thought creatively about funding.

Conclusions

The simulation provoked an increase in performance year-on-year. As experience of working in this environment grew, so did performance. Officers took a little time to understand how to operate in the simulation. The space to think that the simulation created was valuable as was the feedback from experts. Experts tended to see actions as improving in technical quality as time went on. Elements of the trading simulation were vital in encouraging better performance over time. An element of competition, clear targets and encouragement to plan for the future were vital components in increasing the rate of improvement. Also, the financial aspects of the simulation were, for a minority of participants, important in encouraging creative thinking. The simulation forced creativity in later years as pre-planned actions were exhausted for most participants.

The nature of potential

Councils have the potential to make big reductions in CO_2 production across their local areas. What is not yet clear is where this potential lies. The simulation asked councils to consider how their being an estate manager, service provider and placeshaper empowers them to deliver CO_2 savings. To understand how to best wield this potential it is useful to examine which categories of actions achieved the greatest savings. This section analyses the nature of the actions taken by the local authorities and considers what this might tell us about the future local authority role.

Experts and numbers

Experts were offered the opportunity to comment on the individual actions in each year. These comments are essential in assessing the viability of individual actions. In these comments, all experts chose to make reference to specific actions. Many commented positively and noted the probable accuracy of costs and savings.

In other cases, experts were more critical. A small number of suggestions were judged as unrealistic in their technical detail. They might have claimed a much higher CO_2 savings or have estimated much lower cost than would be reasonable. Experts took these outliers into account when making their judgements on CO_2 savings for scoring. When analysing the data, it is important for us to take into account these judgements. Not to do so risks skewing the results of the analysis and, as a result, undermining the validity and reliability of the findings. This section therefore uses the figures presented by the local officers and filtered by experts.

Categorising action

The actions rejected by Expert Panel members as unrealistic are excluded from this analysis. This leaves us with 225 actions for categorisation. We could have divided them into categories designed to reflect their areas of impact within local government established roles. More specifically, we could have compiled groups of 'planning' and 'building energy efficiency' actions.[58]

This approach would have assumed that all the suggested actions would fit within traditional local authority roles. However, the suggestions did not lend themselves to this kind of classification; it is precluded by the nature of the simulation. Officers were asked to consider how the council's influence could be wielded over the whole local area. This suggested that councils had the freedom to be innovative and operate outside the traditional boundaries of local authority action. This second consideration precludes division into the traditional council roles.

This most appropriate classification is the one presented in the Action Audit distributed at the beginning of the simulation. They take account of actions both within and outside of traditional council roles. These categories are as follows:

Estate manager and employer

This category includes actions where the council exercises its direct control over either its assets, such as council buildings, or exercises its direct influence as an employer.

---

[58] NLGN has previously made recommendations on reform to the planning system to encourage householder microgeneration. See Appendix 8 for further details

Service provider

This category includes actions where the council exercises its direct influence through its role as a service provider. This might be through a statutory service, such as education, or discretionary service, such as parking provision.

Placeshaper

This category includes actions that do not fit in the previous two categories. They consist of actions designed to indirectly influence the behaviours of individuals, communities, other parts of the local state and local businesses.

We judged each of the actions against these criteria. This allows us to construct a picture of which actions were the most effective at reducing CO_2 emissions.

Effective actions

The following list presents five actions from the top-ten savers of CO_2 based on the claims of those submitting the suggestions. We have removed those suggestions specifically judged to be outliers by Expert Panel members:

Estate manager and employer *– a total of 50 estate manager and employer actions were submitted over the five rounds, with an average saving for each of 5,432 tonnes.*

- Deliver the Carbon Trust's Local Authority Carbon Management Programme which covers corporate buildings and rented housing stock. This will achieve a 30 per cent reduction in carbon emissions over five years. This would save 100,000 tonnes in a year.

- Conduct an energy efficiency review of all council buildings based on audits to ensure efficient building use. This would include investigating the use of buildings and outdated equipment. Also, it would necessitate correctly setting timer clocks/programmers, space temperatures, and using buildings as they were designed to be used. This would save 20,000 tonnes in a year.

- Council-wide lighting scheme to reduce energy used in council properties. Low energy lamps and automatic controls would be installed. This would save 15,000 tonnes in a year.

- Cut carbon emissions from council buildings by five per cent. This would save 12,000 tonnes in a year.

- Change from an organisation with a high IT carbon footprint to a very low IT carbon footprint. This would be done by modifying systems to reduce the need for IT, procuring low energy systems and equipment and educating staff. This would reduce IT energy consumption by 50 per cent, saving 12,000 tonnes in a year.

Service provider – *a total of 74 service provision actions were submitted over the five rounds at an average saving for each of 23,345 tonnes.*

- Electricity generating scheme linked to landfill sites extended to address remaining 4m tonnes of CO_2 produced from such sites. This would save 500,000 tonnes in a year.

- Create an Energy Service Company to manage the energy requirements of developments in the City Growth Area: 37,500 homes, all built by the end of year five, funded through third party financing. This would save 375,000 tonnes in a year.

- Launch a biomass energy scheme which would include various, woodchip combined heat and power (CHP), energy from waste, and agricultural waste (through anaerobic digestion [AD]) schemes. This would save 200,000 tonnes in a year.

- Construct additional Park and Ride site, which would save 100,000 tonnes in year.

- Start a scheme that halves the amount of waste collected and as a result save 50,000 tonnes in a year.

Placeshaper – *a total of 101 placeshaping actions were submitted over the five rounds at an average saving for each of 61,433 tonnes.*

- Construct 14 Anaerobic Digestion plants to process organic waste, producing energy from methane on two sites in the local area, which would involve working with other local authorities, external partners and influencing the behaviours of local people. The approach would include new Community Schemes, with surplus energy provided to the National Grid. This would save 1,050,000 tonnes in a year.

- Personalised carbon credits for all local residents with each person allocated eight tonnes per year. The scheme would use a 'Carbon Credit Card', and have new meters installed in houses to clock up the amount of electricity used. Cars would be required to use a similar device and flights would also be included within the scheme. This would save 520,000 tonnes in a year.

- Electricity generating scheme linked to landfill sites extended to address remaining 4m tonnes of CO_2 produced from such sites. This would save 500,000 tonnes in a year.

- Establish five District Energy Plants run on wood chip from street trees, parks trees and residents tree waste – providing heat and water to 50 per cent of homes and businesses. This would save 480,000 tonnes in a year.

- ESCO managing energy requirements of developments in a local Growth Area (37,500 homes, all built to be built at end of year five), funded through Third Party Financing (option for financing for the project without the authorities compromising own capital, thus leaving capital available for other priorities). This would save 375,000 tonnes in a year.

Patterns of potential

To understand the potential offered by different types of action it is necessary to understand the potential of each category of action individually. Here, the scores given by experts are unhelpful; they only apply to the full packages of suggestions and cannot be broken down and applied to individual actions in meaningful ways. The research catered for this and was designed to capture data on each action through the self-assessment of local officers.

Each officer was asked to attach judgements on the cost and the savings from each action. However, the expert filter was still in operation; as explained above, some actions were considered to be unrealistic by experts and were removed from the analysis. Figure 14 summarises the average savings made from using each kind of action divided into the three categories. This table uses the figures attached to each action to outline the potential of each area.

This analysis uncovers some striking findings. Using placeshaping was the most prevalent approach to reducing CO_2 emissions when measured by an absolute number of actions – around 45 per cent of suggested actions were in this category. Estate management actions proved to be the least prevalent, with only about 22 per cent of actions falling into this category. Service provision actions were the second most prevalent, representing approximately 30 per cent of

Figure 14 Potential average savings made from each kind of action

Category of action	Number of actions in this area	Proportion of total submitted actions (% of total number)	Proportion of total saving (% tonnes CO_2)	Total savings (ktonnes CO_2)	Average saving per action (ktonnes CO_2)
Estate manager and employer	50	22.2	3	271.61	5.43
Service provider	74	32.9	21	1,727.51	23.35
Placeshaper	101	44.9	76	6,204.71	61.43
Totals	225	n/a	n/a	8,203.83	n/a

actions. This is despite the fact that most council action to date has focused on reducing emissions through taking actions as an estate manager and service provider.

This prevalence can be explained by the size of the savings. Firstly, placeshaping saved by far the most CO_2 – in total, these approaches saved more than two and a half times as much CO_2 as the other kinds of action. Secondly, the average amount saved by each placeshaping action is greater than that saved by actions in the other two categories; more than three and a half times as much as service provision actions and more than twenty-two times as much as estate management actions. Clearly, using the power to placeshape has significantly more potential than focusing solely on driving change through estate management or service provision.

The idea that placeshaping was the most powerful way of reducing emissions was supported by comments made at the feedback meeting. Just reducing emissions from local authority buildings and emissions generated through providing services would not have made the kinds of savings demanded by the simulation. Further, such a constrained approach will not deliver the scale of reductions needed in the real world. Experts and local officers agreed that an approach that involves the whole community as well as local business would be essential in making big, sustained reductions.

Local officers were in agreement that data was essential in influencing communities and businesses. At present, there exists a dearth of data on sub-local authority level CO₂ production patterns. Better data would be essential in designing effective actions in the real world. Even when this data was collected, local officers would need to learn how to use it.

Conclusions

By far the most effective way to reduce CO₂ emissions is to be a placeshaper. Other kinds of actions are essential in establishing the council as an exemplar, but will only ever be a small part of the solution in terms of real-world reductions. This means that local authorities must wield their indirect influence over other parts of the local state, individuals, communities and businesses to provoke changes in behaviour to achieve large savings. The key to realising local government's potential is to empower them to play this role to the fullest extent.

Potential over years

Placeshaping is the most effective way of reducing CO₂ emissions. But it is not yet clear how far performance correlated with the use of placeshaping actions during the simulation. It is useful to examine how the use of different categories of actions changed over time. This will help to reveal at which points placeshaping actions were used. We can then go on to explain reasons for these changes.

It is clear from simulation that wielding indirect influence is the most effective way to make large reductions in CO₂ emissions. It emerged from the feedback meeting that as the simulation progressed and the challenge intensified, so officers sought more ambitious solutions that relied on changing the behaviours of other parts of the local state, communities, individuals and businesses. Other data can test this finding. It is revealing to analyse changes in the composition of packages over time and see whether local officers really did increasingly rely on placeshaping actions as the challenge of reducing CO₂ intensified. Figure 15 makes this comparison.

The comparison reinforces the idea that placeshaping became more important as the challenge intensified. Placeshaping actions were the most prevalent in years two and five when considering the proportion of CO₂ saved by this method. As was revealed in the previous section, 'Performance over time', it was between years one and two and years four and five that performance improved at the fastest rate. This suggests that the way to improve performance is to wield indirect influence across the locality and not to use direct control alone.

Figure 15 Comparison of potential effectiveness between estate managers, service providers and place-shapers

	Year 1	Year 2	Year 3	Year 4	Year 5	Total
Total number of actions	39	39	51	49	47	225
Estate manager	16	12	10	5	7	50
% of number of actions	41.0	30.8	19.6	10.2	14.9	22.2
Annual savings (ktonnes CO_2)	136.02	38.47	30.12	19.97	46.98	271.56
% of CO_2 savings	40.4	5.7	1.6	0.9	1.5	
Service provider	13	12	20	16	13	74
% of number of actions	33.3	30.8	39.2	32.7	27.7	32.9
Annual savings (ktonnes CO_2)	111.08	38.82	476.71	788.97	311.93	1,727.51
% of CO_2 savings	33.0	5.7	25.1	35.8	10.1	
Place-shaper	10	15	21	28	27	101
% of number of actions	25.6	38.5	41.2	57.1	57.4	44.9
Annual savings (ktonnes CO_2)	89.86	602.74	1,393.09	1,395.07	2,723.95	6,204.71
% of CO_2 savings	26.7	88.6	73.3	63.3	88.4	

The proportion of estate management actions reached its zenith in year one and rapidly declined from there. In this first year, 41 per cent of the CO_2 saved came from estate management actions. By year five, this had fallen just under 1.5 per cent. Service provision actions show less of a regular pattern; over a quarter of all CO_2 savings can be attributed to service provision actions in years one, three and four.

This tallies with the findings from the feedback meeting. It was after round one and round four that the local officers felt the most pressure to improve, after year one as very few councils reached their four per cent targets and in year five as the simulation was drawing to an end and the size of the savings to be made was clear. Further, officers saw the need to demonstrate to the local community that they were exemplars of good practice. Appearing to be a beacon of sustainability was an important prerequisite to wielding influence over others. Without picking the 'low-hanging fruit' it would be difficult to have the moral authority needed to lead others' behaviours. Taking placeshaping actions was dependent on being able to demonstrate that the council had borne the burden already.

Conclusions

When the pressure of the simulation began to bite, the solution was to realise CO_2 savings by wielding indirect influence. The bigger the challenge, the more influence was wielded. However, it was still important for local officers to take the simple actions to increasing the energy efficiency of buildings and promote sustainability in local services. It is more likely that a council can wield its influence across the locality if it is able to demonstrate its own sustainability excellence. Tackling emissions within the council's direct control is an important precursor to leading others.

Value for money

The evidence shows that the greatest CO_2 reductions will come from indirectly influencing the behaviours of other parts of the public sector, local business, communities and citizens. However, if the costs of wielding this influence are too large, it seems unlikely that councils will ever be able to fulfil their potential. This section analyses the costs of different kinds of actions and the implications for local government's future role.

Figure 16 compares the average costs per tonne of CO_2 saved of actions in different categories. It omits from the calculations those actions considered to be unrealistic by experts.

Estate management actions were the most expensive, costing around £56 per tonne of CO_2 saved. Service provision actions were less expensive, cost around £45 per tonnes of CO_2 saved. Placeshaping actions were the least expensive, costing around £31 per tonne of CO_2 saved. This is just under half the cost of estate management actions and two thirds of the cost of service provision actions.

Data from the simulation suggests two reasons why placeshaping is the cheapest way of reducing CO_2 emissions. Firstly, in some cases, placeshaping relies solely on changing behaviours. This asks for little or no capital investment. Councils can take advantage of their unique links with local people through targeted publicity campaigns. They can also give targeted advice to householders and local businesses on energy efficiency.

Figure 16 Average costs of actions in different categories per tonne of CO_2 saved

Year	Estate manager	Service provider	Place-shaper	Total number of actions
1	16	13	10	39
2	12	12	15	39
3	10	20	21	51
4	5	16	28	49
5	7	13	27	47
Total actions	50	74	101	225
Savings (ktonnes CO_2)	271,610	1,727,505	6,204,716	8,203,831
Costs (£)	15,261,900	77,601,500	190,712,000	283,575,400
Average saving per action (ktonnes CO_2)	5,432	23,345	61,433	36,461
Average cost of action (£)	305,238	1,048,669	1,888,238	1,260,335
Average cost per tonne	56.19	44.92	30.74	34.57

Secondly, placeshaping allows the cost of making CO_2 savings to be spread across partners. Many of the suggestions showed contributions from sources other than the council that would lead to cost savings for businesses and individuals. As a result, neither the cost nor the savings are restricted to the council. The local authority is the leader rather than the deliverer.

An alternative explanation is that participating officers are underestimating the cost of placeshaping actions or overestimating the cost of estate management and service provision actions. However, these suggestions have been passed through the expert filter and those considered to be unrealistic rejected from the analysis. Generalisations from these figures gives a useful indication of costs in the three areas of action.

Conclusions

Local authorities have numerous avenues available to them to tackle climate change. It is clear that placeshaping actions offer the most cost-effective way of reducing CO_2 emissions. Placeshaping allows costs to be best spread across partners. Savings can also be made for all those involved. Revenue can also be generated by taking innovative approaches to cutting emissions. When taking placeshaping actions, neither costs nor savings are restricted to the council. The local authority does not have to invest heavily to lead.

Meeting targets

Being a placeshaper allows councils to take cost-effective actions that will reduce CO_2 emissions across the locality. Wielding indirect influence over local partners, communities and citizens offers the most potential for making savings. Aspects of the trading simulation helped to encourage improving performance between years. Competition, clear targets and incentives to construct coherent strategies all encouraged officers to do better. It is useful to compare the potential of local authorities to existing and future targets. This will give an indication of how far local government can be a part of a national solution to the climate change challenge.

Figure 17 makes comparisons between NLGN's simulation and the targets contained in three important documents that seek to establish a framework for reducing CO_2 emissions.

The data from the simulation is divided into two columns. The first gives results for the whole of the simulation. The second gives the results of the most successful council. Subsequent columns refer to real-world targets; the first set are contained in the draft UK Climate Change Bill. This is represented by two separate columns, one that refers to the interim 2020 target and the other the overarching 2050 target. The second outlines a hypothetical Climate Change Act that sets out more challenging targets.[59] The third is the London Climate Change Action Plan from the London Climate Change Agency which sets even more ambitious targets for the city.

---

59 The 80 per cent figure reflects the conclusions of a recent Parliamentary committee that found that it understood and had sympathy with, '…the argument in favour of setting a higher target for the long-term reduction of carbon dioxide emissions,' although did not recommend that the target be raised to 80 per cent. Joint Committee on the Draft Climate Change Bill, *Draft Climate Change Bill* (3 August 2007), Section 7, p 76

Figure 17 London climate change action plan targets

	NLGN simulation – whole market	NLGN simulation – most successful LA7	UK draft Climate Change Bill 1st phase	UK draft Climate Change Bill 2nd phase	UK draft Climate Change Bill – possible change	Mayor of London's Climate Change Action Plan
Total target reductions (% CO₂)	20% below 2004 baseline CO₂ levels	20% below 2004 baseline CO₂ levels	26% below 1990 baseline CO₂ levels	34% below 1990 baseline CO₂ levels	80% below 1990 baseline CO₂ levels	60% below 1990 baseline CO₂ levels
Dates within which to be achieved	2008 to 2013	2008 to 2013	2008 to 2020	2020 to 2050	2008 to 2050	2007 to 2025
Required average annual reductions (% CO₂ from baseline)	4	4	2.2	1.1	1.9	4
Actual annual reductions (% CO₂ from baseline)	3.56	5.6	n/a	n/a	n/a	n/a

These comparisons are revealing. The evidence suggests that, given the right environment within which to operate, actions led by local authorities can meet and exceed the legally binding targets that the Government will soon bring forward in legislation. If the average rate of reduction from the simulation can be sustained over a period of years, councils have the potential to reduce CO_2 emissions from the 2004 baseline by 60 per cent by 2025 and make 80 per cent reductions by 2031. If the average performance of the most effective authority can be mirrored in other authorities, councils offer to meet the 60 per cent target by 2019 and the 80 per cent target by 2023.[60]

---

60 These figures assume that reductions will begin in 2008 and be sustained at the average level

This would outstrip the demands of the legally binding target that the Government intends to introduce, whether a 60 or an 80 per cent reduction target for domestic emissions[61] is eventually included in the legislation. The Royal Society for Arts believes that a mandatory personal carbon scheme can be introduced by 2013.[62] Assuming that this will happen, local government offers to reduce CO_2 emissions by over 22 per cent by this date if the performance of all authorities can match the performance of the most successful during the simulation. It is also in excess of even London's ambitious plans. The dominant unknown here would be the extent to which rates of reductions changed over time. If levels were to drop after five years, this would have a major effect on the potential of local government to deliver these demanding targets.

However, the simulation gives grounds to expect that performance might continue to improve when measured across all councils. As the earlier section reveals, performance during the simulation improved year-on-year with varying rates of change between years. More CO_2 was saved each year than in the previous year. If councils can continue this improvement over a longer period than five years, they would make even faster progress towards creating a low carbon economy.

At present, the draft Climate Change Bill makes no reference to the Government's recognition of this potential. The Committee on Climate Change will not include those from local government with practical experience of reducing CO_2 emissions. The long-term 60 per cent reduction target is 'front-loaded', meaning that more CO_2 would have to be saved in earlier years rather than later ones.

Our research suggests that councils should be at the heart of the fight against climate change. They can use their placeshaping potential to achieve bigger savings than outlined in even the most ambitious public sector plans. Further, local government might remove the need to 'front-load' the savings to be made under the Climate Change Bill. Councils actually get better at reducing emissions over time, not worse.

Conclusions

The findings from the simulation, filtered by independent sustainability experts, show that local authorities can deliver CO_2 savings more quickly than any existing or proposed set of targets, if the performance of the whole can be brought up to the level of the most successful. If the average rate of reduction identified in the

---

61 Government figures exclude CO_2 emissions from aviation, shipping and offshore gas and oil emissions
62 www.rsacarbonlimited.org/viewarticle.aspa?pageid=797&nodeid=1

scenario is maintained, local government offers to reduce CO_2 by 60 per cent by 2025. It might be possible to make these savings even faster if performance continues to increase over time. Empowering councils might not necessitate 'front-loading' savings targets as in the Climate Change Bill. The government has the opportunity to use the upcoming Climate Change Bill to create a system that encourages local authorities to make the most of its potential.

Expert versus local view

The analysis so far has used two different sets of figures to reveal the potential of local government; one set from experts and the other from self-assessment. To evaluate the validity and reliability of the research, it is useful to compare these figures and to account for differences.

The simulation generated two separate figures for CO_2 savings; the one used to score the annual returns and one resulting from officer self-assessment. These figures also allow us to compare the views of expert panel members and the claims of local authority officers. The suggestions marked as unrealistic by experts have again been removed from the local officer figures. Figure 18 makes the comparison.

It reveals a difference in the scale of the savings claimed by local officers and those allocated by experts. In total, experts scored the packages of suggestions at approximately 81 per cent of the final figure claimed by local officers. This shows that local officers, on average, were over-claiming the amount of CO_2 that their actions would save. This suggests that the simulation gave incentives to overestimate the level of savings in order to gain a higher score and achieve targets.

Figure 18 Comparison for CO_2 savings between expert and local officer views

	Total (expert)	Total (local officers)
Year 1	500.56	336.95
Year 2	1,066.30	680.03
Year 3	1,441.96	1,899.97
Year 4	1,556.59	2,204.02
Year 5	2,100.28	3,082.86
Total	**6,665.69**	**8,203.83**

Changes over the five years are also revealing. In years one and two, local officers tended to underestimate the size of CO_2 savings their packages would make. By year three local officers were overestimating the level of savings their suggestions would make. This trend continued in years four and five. It is likely that officers became increasingly optimistic about the levels of savings that their suggestions would make as they moved out of the familiar territory of improving energy efficiency in council buildings and towards schemes designed to influence communities and individuals. It is worth noting that local officers were asked to construct packages of actions stretching five years into the future and in areas of which they have little experience.

It is therefore reasonable to conclude that officers were keen to show their suggestions in the best possible lights and achieve the highest possible savings in the final three rounds of the simulation. In round one and two it might be that officers underestimated savings in areas of which they had most experience. This overall difference could also be due to unfamiliarity with the scenario presented in the simulation and a lack of experience in taking actions that would influence outside of those areas of direct control. If this is the case, it is likely that the accuracy with which officers forecast savings would grow over time as experience, and therefore capabilities, increased.

Comments made at the final feedback meeting support the idea that accuracy suffered as the challenge intensified. As officers were required to use more placeshaping actions to reduce CO_2 emissions, it became harder to know what would be the savings achieved. Part of the reason is that most councils do not have the data they require to accurately assess the impacts of community-level actions. Officers were unanimous in their perception that wielding influence over local communities would require better data.

Conclusions

The differences in the self-assessments and expert assessments reveals a lack of experience among local officers of wielding influence. Councils need better data on the production of CO_2 across their localities as well as the probable effects on their target audience. In a real-world situation where local authorities are asked to make big savings in CO_2 emissions, it also suggests that there should be third party assessment of the claims made for reductions. Not to have such assessments would risk creating an inaccurate picture of progress in reducing CO_2 emissions.

Political viability

It is commonly believed that measures designed to reduce CO_2 production will prove unpopular with politicians, businesses and citizens. The simulation was designed to assess the political impacts of tackling climate change by asking local officers to assess each individual suggestion for political viability. This section examines the findings from this part of the research and reveals how political favourability changes over time.

These political judgements were also passed through an expert political filter. This person was asked to comment on each of the suggestions and make a judgement on the political assessment made by officers. None of the suggestions marked as politically favourable by local officers were considered so outlandish as to be impossible by our political expert. As a result, none have been omitted from this analysis. However, suggestions previously judged as technically unfeasible by other expert panel members have been omitted. Figure 19 summarises changes in local officer judgements on political viability over time.

Contrary to popular perception, by the end of the simulation, political favourability had grown from its starting point. Over 85 per cent of actions were considered favourable in the final year compared with only 72 per cent in year one. However, year one was not the zenith of unpopularity; in fact, year three was. Almost one fifth of actions in this year were considered to be politically unfavourable. This can be explained by how officers structured their actions. Many ran over a number of years, starting as politically unfavourable, becoming

Figure 19 Changes in local officer judgements on political viability over time

	Round 1	Round 2	Round 3	Round 4	Round 5	Total
Total number of actions	39	39	51	49	47	
Favourable	28	32	28	40	40	74.7%
%	71.8	82.1	68.3	81.6	85.1	
Neutral	38	3	6	6	7	13.3%
%	20.5	7.7	14.6	12.2	14.9	
Unfavourable	3	4	7	3	0	7.6%
%	7.7	10.3	17.1	6.1	0.0	

neutral and ending as favourable. Councils were required to show political leadership and take risks in order to reap the political benefits in time.

There is a striking correlation between performance, the use of placeshaping actions and political favourability. In the years when placeshaping actions were most prevalent, years two and five, political impacts were at their most favourable. Further, these are the same two years that experienced the biggest improvement in performance over the previous year. It seems that the greater the impact on climate change and the more the council seeks to influence local people the more political capital there is to be gained. Tackling climate change should therefore be near the top of every administration's list.

Conclusions

Political capital can be built by tackling climate change. Contrary to popular perception, measures that reduce CO_2 emissions need not upset voters and jeopardise the positions of politicians. On the contrary, the faster the rate of progress in reducing CO_2 emissions the greater the benefit. Also, the more the council seeks to wield indirect influence, the more political capital there is to be gained.

Trading and cost-effectiveness

The simulation was designed to make participants consider the cost-effectiveness of their actions. They were asked to include judgements on the financial cost of each action in their submissions. As part of the annual feedback, participants were informed of how much they would have spent on carbon credits had they not made the CO_2 savings they did. This allowed officers to compare the costs of their actions with the cost of not making CO_2 savings. This comparison allowed for a judgement on cost-effectiveness.

The simulation created virtual financial incentives for officers to reduce CO_2 emissions. The trading aspect of the simulation was designed to persuade officers to consider the cost-effectiveness of the actions they suggested. Trading gave CO_2 price according to hypothetical developments outlined in Analyst's Bulletin issued for every year of the simulation. These bulletins are included in Appendix 4. As part of their annual feedback, officers were given the figures that compared the cost of their actions to the cost of carbon credits they otherwise would have had to buy to cover the same amount of CO_2. This gave them the numbers to balance the cost of taking action against the cost of inaction in an environment where inaction had a price.

This allowed officers to calculate whether simply buying carbon credits would have been more cost-effective than taking action to reduce CO_2 emissions. From these figures they were able to judge how much finance was available every year that could be spent on reducing CO_2 emissions. Actions that cost vastly more than the price of the CO_2 they saved would not be viable as they would financially disadvantage the council. Actions that cost significantly less than the equivalent CO_2 price would put them at a financial advantage.

The cost of CO_2 was based on real-world examples as discussed in the research design chapter. The simulation expressed the price as a carbon credit, which represented one tonne of CO_2. We intended to increase the cost of carbon over the five years, starting with levels seen during the EU Emissions Trading Scheme towards the roughly £42 per tonne figure suggested by Stern as the social cost of CO_2.

We predetermined the cost of credits before the simulation began. But participants were only made vaguely aware of future prices. They were given predictions on the future cost of carbon credits both in the next year and by the end of the simulation. Hypothetical external events were introduced during the simulation to justify fluctuations in price. For example, year three saw a major new entrant into the world energy markets. Suddenly, long-term supplies of fossil fuels were greatly increased, leading to a sharp and sustained drop in energy prices. People started to consume more fossil fuels. This led to greater competition for carbon credits among local authorities to match the rise in the locality's CO_2 footprint, increasing the market price of credits.

There was little chance that officers might choose to just buy carbon credits and take no action to reduce CO_2 emissions; the scenario placed a legal duty on councils to make reductions. So, even if officers did not grasp the unfamiliar concept of cost-effectiveness, the research would not be undermined. Figure 20 overleaf demonstrates the results across all seven local authorities over the five years of the simulation. The costs and savings from actions judged to be unfeasible by expert panel members are again excluded from these figures.

The graph reveals the extent to which the group of councils achieved cost-effectiveness over the five years of the simulation. Where the dark line is above the light line, officers have spent more on actions to reduce CO_2 than they would

Figure 20 Cost-effectiveness across all seven local authorities over the five years of the simulation

Year	Costs estate management (£000s)	Costs service provision (£000s)	Costs placeshaping (£000s)	Total cost of actions (£000s)	Cost of CO_2 per tonne (£)	Equivalent cost of CO_2 (£000s)
1	5,890	2,528	12,895	21,313	18.00	9,010
2	1,345	29,248	10,521	41,114	21.60	23,032
3	967	24,298	56,036	81,301	29.70	42,826
4	517	10,839	62,165	73,521	33.00	51,367
5	6,542	10,689	49,095	66,326	40.00	84,011
TOTAL	15,262	77,602	190,712	283,575	n/a	210,247

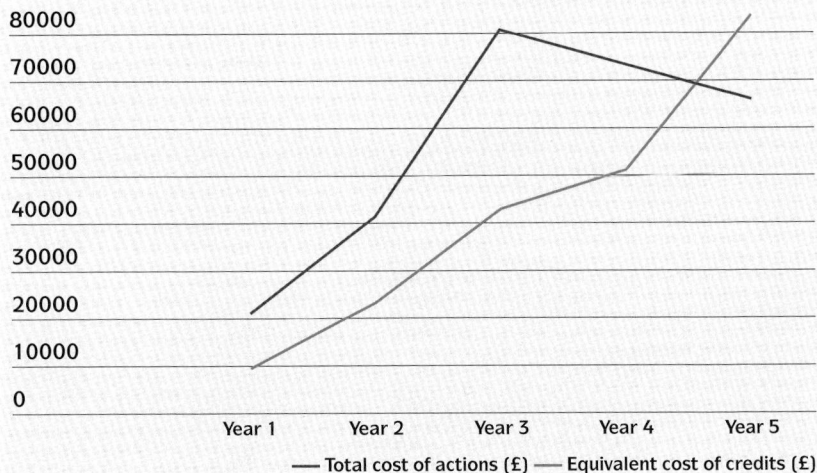

otherwise have spent on carbon credits to save the same amount of CO_2 . Where the light line is below the dark line, local authorities have spent less on actions to reduce CO_2 than they would otherwise have spent on credits if they had done nothing.

The group was not cost-effective in the first three years. Cost-ineffectiveness peaked in year three. In this year, councils spent close to double on taking action than they would otherwise have spent on carbon credits to save the same amount of CO_2. In year four, the group remained cost ineffective, although by a smaller margin than in year three. By year five, the group had become cost-effective. They were spending less on actions to reduce CO_2 than they otherwise would have been required to spend on carbon credits to cover the amount of CO_2 saved.

This suggests a number of findings; firstly that the mid-simulation feedback distributed to participant councils at the end of year three had an effect on attitudes to cost-effectiveness. This feedback showed that councils were not being cost-effective. It seems likely that this helped to clarify the purpose of the trading element and the meaning of cost-effectiveness. Comments from participants made during the simulation suggest that the trading element was unfamiliar to officers. Seeing cost-effectiveness represented as a graph helped officers to understand the importance of trading within the simulation.

Findings from the final feedback meeting support this view. Few officers considered the cost-effectiveness of their actions when constructing packages of suggestions at any point of the game. Most simply constructed packages of suggestions that would meet the targets, more so in the earlier than the later rounds. For the minority that did take finance into consideration, it was a powerful driver. As one participant commented, he began the simulation thinking like a sustainability officer and ended it thinking like a venture capitalist. Those that achieved cost-effectiveness constructed packages that levered in external finance and generated revenue.

From this we can conclude that officers are more familiar with legal and regulatory imperatives than financial incentives. Officers are most used to seeking funding from various national or supra-national funding pots. They tend to raise money to pay for schemes that have already been designed rather than designing schemes that have innovative methods of finance at their core. Operating in an environment where they are asked to calculate cost-effectiveness and make decisions on the merits of various schemes based on the ratio of how much they cost to how much CO_2 they save is unfamiliar.

It seems increasingly likely that sustainability professionals will have to work in a world where carbon has a price. The uncertainty is about how this price will be determined and applied. This future requires that council environmental departments develop the financial skills and competencies required to deliver on their potential to reduce CO_2 emissions. Improved skills will empower officers to invest in actions that, over a period of time, would be cost neutral to the council and therefore would not require extra local tax revenue.

Conclusions

The concept of trading and its financial aspects are not familiar to local environment officers. Explanation of what cost-effectiveness is helped to improve financial performance. Those that did consider cost-effectiveness were incentivised to take creative approaches to finance. In a world where carbon has a price, financial competence will become increasingly important. It will become increasingly important for local environment officers to have financial skill in order to take advantage of this potential.

5 *Conclusions and recommendations*

Local government can take responsibility for reducing domestic emissions.[63] Our research reveals that if the performance of the best local authorities can be matched, councils can reduce CO₂ production by 60 per cent by 2019. This is 31 years before central government expects to reach this level of saving. This is a powerful offer that should not be ignored.

This potential is borne of local government's unique placeshaping role. Councils have the democratic legitimacy to bring together local public bodies, businesses and communities in partnerships. They also offer to influence how citizens behave. Tackling climate change through placeshaping offers value for money and has the biggest potential for CO₂ savings. Further, the research revealed that the tougher the challenge, the more placeshaping becomes vital in reducing emissions. Councils respond well to the pressure of tough targets.

Placeshaping is dependent on moral authority. Councils must become exemplars of sustainability to be able to influence the behaviour of others. Reducing emissions from council buildings and embedding sustainability in services are vital precursors to exercising leadership. The council must be viewed as a beacon of good practice.

The research also revealed the important roles that targets, competition and finance play in driving improvement. Targets give officers clear goals and benchmarks against which success can be measured. A sense of competition between peers encourages better performance. Consideration of the cost-effectiveness of actions to tackle climate change encourages officers to be creative in their approaches. Together, these led to sustained improvement in performance over time.

The research also considered the political implications of tackling climate change at the local level. Without political support, action would be likely to fail. The simulation revealed that tackling climate change is overwhelmingly politically popular under the right circumstances. Councils are also capable of winning

---

63 'Domestic' refers to all UK emissions excluding shipping, domestic aviation and offshore oil & gas

approval for new local regulations. Long-term actions tended to grow in popularity over time as the benefits were realised. This suggests that strong and bold political leadership is key to realising local government's potential.

Yet the present system is not designed to capture the benefits of this potential. The following recommendations are designed to remove barriers and empower the whole of the state to rise to the climate change challenge.

Funding and finance

Suitable levels and methods of funding are vital components of building viable approaches to tackling climate change. At present, the funding system does not encourage the long-term capital investment necessary to make big CO_2 reductions even where these have strongly beneficial whole-life economics. Further, local authorities have proved reluctant to use funding freedoms available to them to finance capital investment.

However, simply increasing the level of central government funding for local government to tackle climate change is unrealistic; either funding would have to be cut elsewhere or the overall tax burden would have to increase. Neither are viable options at this time of tightening budgets. Instead, the Government could create a fiscally neutral solution that empowers local authorities to take responsibility for their own finances. The first step would be to establish the long-term reduction target in legislation as the Government is currently proposing:

- **the Government should continue on its current path and create new legally binding targets to reduce CO_2 emissions by 60 per cent of 1990 levels by 2050 across the UK**.

This will establish a baseline from which to work. However, it will not be enough to actually achieve savings. Councils should be empowered to take practical action.

New funding mechanisms

As the evidence shows, councils have the potential to achieve these savings in less time. The simulation also revealed that some aspects of a trading system would create new incentives for councils to reduce CO_2 emissions. Incentives born of targets, competition and finance came together to create a powerful set of drivers. This might suggest that carbon trading is the vehicle for rising to the climate change challenge.

However, such a scheme would have drawbacks. Firstly, it would present an as yet unknown set of challenges to local officers. Council would be required to rapidly hone a wide range of financial skills. Or, councils would be required to buy in these skills. Either way, the process would be lengthy and potentially expensive. Secondly, it would be potentially over-complex for both officers and local politicians. The scale of the climate change challenge demands immediate action.

Instead, the Government could create a new system that would capture the benefits of carbon trading without the complexity. Additional funding should be allocated on the basis of improvement above national minimum standards. This could be achieved by introducing the following measures:

- **establish through negotiation a target for CO_2 reduction for each local authority to be managed through the Local Area Agreement (LAA) – these targets should reflect the levels of savings enshrined in the Government's 2050 target**.

Routing funding through LAAs will also allow councils to take the lead in pooling resources across the local state. Using LAAs and their partner bodies, Local Strategic Partnerships (LSPs), allows councils to bring together different policy strands and funding streams that emanate from national government departments at the local level. Strengthened LAAs and LSPs also offer the possibility of working more effectively with the businesses central to tackling climate change, such as energy companies and utilities.

But challenging targets and local joining-up would not necessarily drive improvement. The Government could choose to:

- **attach a performance grant to CO_2 reduction targets that would establish individual CO_2 reduction targets for each council**; and

- **establish long-term financial penalties and rewards that would financially reward overachievement and penalise underachievement**.

    This could work as follows:

    - for every percentage point saved above the target, the council would receive a fixed payment; and

- for every percentage point below the agreed reduction target, the council would be required to pay the same fixed amount to central government[64]

This system assumes that some CO_2 savings can be made by councils within existing budgets. A number of trail-blazing councils have already proven themselves capable. But the pace of CO_2 reduction has not been fast enough to meet the size of the challenge.

More rapid improvement would unlock new finance to be invested in reducing CO_2 emissions. However, since the performance grant is retrospective, ambitious councils would be required to raise their own finance secured on future revenue. This could be done in two ways – either:

- **use loan finance from central government raised via the prudential borrowing regime through the Public Works Loan Board** (this has the advantage of being an inexpensive way of raising finance); or

- **raise private sector capital** (this would have the advantage of applying a high level of commercial discipline to the loan – it would potentially have the disadvantage of being relatively expensive).[65]

It would be down to each council to choose the most appropriate financing option. Councils would also have the option to raise finance through CO_2 reduction schemes. As the research has shown, some approaches to reducing CO_2 can generate their own revenue. Also, placeshaping has the potential to lever-in finance from other bodies; public and private sector.

This approach would mean that the whole of the state can achieve its target of 60 per cent CO_2 reductions by 2050. The approach is cost neutral where negotiations allow each party to reach realistic targets. It would also replicate the three main drivers of improvement from the research simulation; targets, competition and finance.

Managing finance in this way would do away with the need for new top-down climate change performance indicators to be built into the performance regime.

---

64 These rewards would have to allow the level of rewards and penalties to vary between councils according to the level of challenge in each area. Some will find it harder than others to reduce the area's CO_2 footprint. A baseline figure to work from would be Stern's judgement on the social cost of CO_2

65 The Government would have to be clear on its commitment to providing the performance grant at the level agreed at the beginning of the process. To renege on the agreement would jeopardise a council's financial position

The responsibility for delivering improved performance would be devolved to individual local authorities. Penalties for underperformance would be financial rather than regulatory. The model assumes that improvement is a minimum requirement and that only more rapid improvement should be rewarded.

This approach would also offer local politicians the possibility of realising the political benefits of tackling climate change. More local financial freedom will empower local executives to take responsibility for measures that will impact over a period of years. As the research has shown, strong political leadership promises to deliver electoral advantages.

Exploring trading

New financial arrangements could replicate the benefits and market discipline of a trading system. But it might be that in the long-term inter-authority carbon trading offers a more complete set of drivers to persuade local authorities to take advantage of their potential. A trading system would require similar targets as a regulatory system, but would allow for even more tangible competition and stronger financial drivers. Price and competitive pressures would be brought on bear on a daily basis.

However, it is likely that such a scheme would take time to construct and require considerable investment to gain mindshare in councils. The Government could therefore:

- **commission a wide-ranging inter-authority carbon trading simulation involving a large number of councils and operating over a period of time**.

A more extensive simulation offers to reveal detail on the future operation of inter-authority carbon trading and inform any future pilot schemes.

- **DEFRA, the Department for Communities and Local Government (DCLG) and the devolved administrations should use these findings to launch pilot schemes to test these findings across local government**.

Removing obstacles to local energy schemes

The simulation revealed that one of the most significant roles that councils can play in creating a low carbon economy is by being the catalyst for local combined heat and power schemes.[66] The matching of heat sinks in the community to by-

---

[66] As Appendix 6 shows, a large number of community energy and Energy Service Company (ESCO) schemes are suggested by a wide range of participants.

product heat from electrical power generation can have a dramatic effect on CO_2 emissions when compared to centralised electricity generation and distribution. The development of this market is important to the delivery of embedded energy.

However, there is at present a slow rate of progress in this market which should be addressed. Councils can face challenges in negotiating appropriate pricing for the electricity flows into and out of the electricity grid. Councils and arms-length ESCOs face an unhelpful regulatory framework for electricity with which embedded energy schemes must interface. As a result, the Government could:

• **amend the regulatory framework to facilitate the growth of the ESCO market to enable local authorities to accelerate delivery of embedded energy**.

Improving skills and competencies

Using a regulatory approach that devolves a part of the national target to each local authority makes two assumptions: firstly, that councils and central government have the negotiation skills required to agree mutually satisfactory targets. But this might not be the case everywhere. To cater for this, civil servants and local officers should be supported in improving their negotiation skills by the Improvement and Development Agency (IDeA) or a similar body.

Secondly, setting the right reduction targets would also depend on the skills and competencies of local environment officers. Realistic targets are only possible where councils know how, by how much and at what expense CO_2 can be reduced. The research has shown that these skills need to be improved to bring all councils up to the level of the best. This might be achieved by:

• **establishing roving teams of local sustainability experts to be employed on a consultancy basis by councils. These experts should be drawn from exemplar local authorities with track records of success, commercial finance and community-based environmental entrepreneurs. These teams could be co-ordinated through IDeA**.

Such measures could empower local authorities to be confident in their capacity to borrow against future financial gains. However, these teams are unlikely to give officers the levels of financial skill necessary to successfully design and manage all the financial aspects of tackling climate change. More financial experience will be necessary. Local authorities already have this level of financial expertise. Councils could choose to:

- develop plans shared between Finance and Environment departments for taking advantage of the flexibility offered by new performance grants.

Gathering better data

However, developing new systems for finance and improving skills and competencies will not give councils the full toolkit they need to reach their potential. As the research uncovered, a lack of appropriate data hinders the placeshaping role. Such an approach requires a detailed understanding of emission patterns across local communities, local businesses and the wider local state. The following measures could help to create the data sets required:

- LGA to establish a commission to develop better statistics. This commission would inform DEFRA on how to improve the experimental statistics on CO_2 emissions by local authority area so they accurately complied sub-ward level data. This commission would include experts from local government.

Climate Change Bill

This legislation could contain measures that reinforce local government's role in reducing CO_2 emissions:

- all reductions in domestic emissions of CO_2 to be attributed to local government, bar those from offshore oil and gas, domestic aviation and shipping.

Attributing reductions in this way would be a powerful statement of intent from the Government. It would suggest that the local government family would have a responsibility similar to that of ministers for reporting progress against the long-term reduction target. This would suggest:

- the Chair of the LGA should be responsible for reporting to Parliament on progress against target on an annual basis alongside Ministers.

The Committee on Climate Change will be the body charged with the responsibility for developing solutions that will help the whole of the state to reach its emissions target. In this new environment having expert representation from local authorities would be important. LGA could be charged with the responsibility of delegating council experts to the committee. Also, as all CO_2

reductions will be allocated to local authorities, it would be reasonable to base the Committee at the LGA as a permanent Commission.

Executive commitment

These measures could remove many of the practical barriers to councils achieving their full potential to reduce CO_2 emissions. However, perceptual barriers would remain. Local government is still seen by some as incapable of delivering on big policy challenges. Our research reveals the inaccuracy of this perception. To reinforce the role of local government, the national executive could make a public statement:

• **on passing of the Climate Change Act, the Prime Minister could make a statement on local government's essential role in delivering solutions to the climate change challenge**.

Together, these reforms could empower local government to take the lead in tackling climate change. The prize is for the whole of the state to work together to rise to the climate change challenge.

Appendix 1 *Contributors*

The time, commitment and expertise of the participants were vital in the research process. The contributions of the following people were essential in making the field work a success:

Dominic Allen *Sustainability Manager, Norfolk County Council*

Dr Catherine Bottrill *Oxford University, Environmental Change Institute*

Dr Christian Brand *Oxford University, Environmental Change Institute*

Abigail Burridge *Sustainability Officer, London Borough of Havering*

Graeme Cameron *Assurance and Sustainability Manager, Serco*

Jessica Currie *Sustainable Development Policy Officer, London Borough of Lambeth*

Dr Stewart Davies *Managing Director, Government Facilities Management, Serco*

Dr Tina Fawcett Oxford University, Environmental Change Institute

Brooke Flanagan *Strategy Manager, Energy Savings Trust*

Philip Hume *Head of Policy and Governance, Kirklees Council*

Kevin Jones *Head of Environmental Strategy Branch, Essex County Council*

Debbie King *Environment Policy Officer, Lancashire County Council*

Chris Leslie *Director, New Local Government Network*

Clementine Ludford *WRE Environmental Project Officer, Essex County Council*

Lynn Mapley *Design and Project Management, Sheffield City Council*

Clare Phillips *Environment Policy Team Leader, Lancashire County Council*

Shadia Rahman *Environmental Protection Officer, Middlesbrough Council*

Tim Rogers *Principal Energy Engineer, Sheffield City Council*

Ian Smith *Managing Director, Community Energy Plus*

Phil Webber *Head of Environment Unit, Kirklees Council*

Appendix 2 *Simulation timetable*

Round 1	**Mon 25 June**	**9am**	**Year 1 begins**
	Tues 26 June	**4pm**	*Deadline* – Year 1 returns from councils to NLGN **Year 1 ends**
		5pm	Suggestions to Expert Panel members
	Wed 27 June	**5pm**	*Deadline* – Expert Panel returns to NLGN
Round 2	**Thur 28 June**	**9am**	**Year 2 begins** NLGN feedback to councils, inc. Analyst Bulletin
	Fri 29 June	**4pm**	*Deadline* – Year 2 returns from councils to NLGN **Year 2 ends**
		5pm	Suggestions to Expert Panel members
	Mon 2 July	**5pm**	*Deadline* – Expert Panel returns to NLGN
Round 3	**Tues 3 July**	**9am**	**Year 3 begins** NLGN feedback to councils, inc. Analyst Bulletin
	Wed 4 July	**4pm**	*Deadline* – Year 2 returns from councils to NLGN **Year 3 ends**
		5pm	Suggestions to Expert Panel members
	Thurs 5 July	**5pm**	*Deadline* – Expert Panel returns to NLGN
Round 4	**Friday 6 July**	**9am**	**Year 4 begins** NLGN feedback to councils, inc. Analyst Bulletin
	Monday 9 July	**4pm**	*Deadline* – Year 4 returns from councils to NLGN **Year 4 ends**
		5pm	Suggestions to Expert Panel members
	Tues 10 July	**5pm**	*Deadline* – Expert Panel returns to NLGN
Round 5	**Wed 11 July**	**9am**	**Year 4 begins** NLGN feedback to councils, inc. Analyst Bulletin
	Thurs 12 July	**4pm**	*Deadline* – Year 4 returns from councils to NLGN **Year 5 ends**
		5pm	Suggestions to Expert Panel members
	Fri 13 July	**5pm**	*Deadline* – Expert Panel returns to NLGN

Appendix 3 *Returns form*

Playing the Carbon Game			
Authority and Officer Names:	Round number: 1		
Description of carbon reduction action:	Estimated cost (£)	Estimated saving (tonnes)	Estimated Political Impact (favourable, neutral, or unfavourable)
Assessment of impact of actions from last round:	Total:	Total:	
n/a for Year 1			
For Expert Panel Use Only:			
	Feasibility:	% Change:	Expert Score:
	5	-8	
	4	-6	
	3	-4	
	2	-2	
	1	0	

Appendix 4 *Example feedback email*

The following is a typical example of the email sent to research participants at the end of each year of the simulation:

This email marks the beginning of Year 4 of the carbon trading simulation. Your suggestions from Year 3 have been assessed by our Expert Panel members and the results are in. Expert Panel members were asked to assess your overall package of suggestions according to their technical and political viability. Panel members then gave the full package a simple score that we have translated into a carbon saving. Most importantly, please remember, this is a game! The results of the assessment are as follows:

- Estimated carbon saving – 104.81 kilotonnes

- Estimated cost (£) of carbon savings – £3.62 million

- Equivalent cost (£) of credits to cover the carbon amount – £3.11 million

Your package of suggestions for Year 3 was also assessed for technical and political viability. The following is a summary of the comments:

- Technical – This is an excellent range of innovative schemes and practical suggestions that would have a significant impact on the local area's carbon footprint. The internal carbon trading scheme is of particular interest as, although it would not necessarily save the most carbon in this year, it could provoke a significant shift in organisational culture and embed the principles of sustainability across the local authority.

- Political – A well-balanced and thoroughly considered package of reforms that would take advantage of many of the council's avenues of influence. It is impressive that the package includes a forward mapping exercise that would lay the groundwork for success in the future, and therefore increase the potential for favourable political response.

In Year 4, you are again asked to balance the cost of credits with the cost of actions that will reduce carbon emissions. Government has again chosen to reduce the number of credits available in the market by 4 per cent. This reduction sets a 4 per cent target for each local area. You are asked to make local actions as cost-effective as possible. Your carbon baseline for Year 4 is 1,310 kilotonnes.

Also, attached to this email is a 'Start of Year' Analyst's Bulletin looking back at Year 3 and looking forward to Year 4. It takes a brief look at events outside the control of the local authority that might affect the price of carbon credits. It also gives a forecast price for Year 4 and a long-term forecast of the price of carbon credits.

N.B. The next deadline for returns is Monday 9 July, 4 pm.

Appendix 5 *Analyst's bulletins*

Each annual feedback email was accompanied by an Analyst's Bulletin. This outlined the events that impacted on the price of credits in previous years and that might impact in the following year. We produce no bulletin for year five as feedback was given orally at the feedback meeting at NLGN. The four bulletins follow:

Playing the Carbon Game

Start of Year – Analyst's Bulletin

++

Last Year (Year 1)

The estimated carbon price for Year 1 was £18 per tonne. This estimate has proven accurate. This is because Year 1 was a relatively stable year: Gas supplies were in line with analysts' expectations, the price of oil remained within predicted bounds, Government's plans for new regulation unfolded as expected, and the renewable energy market continued its steady growth in size. As a result, energy costs for citizens and organisations remained relatively constant.

This price stability for energy led to stability in the UK local authority carbon credit market. Local authorities were able to predict with accuracy the demand for energy, and therefore carbon, in their local areas.

++

Next Year (Year 2)

Government has reduced the supply of carbon credits in the market by four per cent. This reduction will likely lead to increased competition for carbon credits putting pressure on prices.

Energy markets are widely predicted to be as stable in Year 2 as they were in Year 1. Gas and oil supplies are predicted to remain consistent and the role of renewable energy will continue to grow.

However, there is a rumour of a major new entrant into the international energy market. If this were to happen, energy prices could be depressed. But all things remaining equal, analysts predict carbon credit prices will rise in line with expectations to £21.60 per tonne in Year 2. Government anticipates that by the end of the 5th year of carbon trading the credit price will rise to around £35.

Playing the Carbon Game

Start of Year – Analyst's Bulletin

++

Last Year (Year 2)

The estimated carbon price for Year 2 was £21.60 per tonne. This estimate has proven accurate. Prices on the international energy markets in Year 2 were again relatively stable despite earlier expectations of a major new entrant into the international energy market. The renewable energy market continued its steady growth in size.

This price stability for energy led to stability in the UK local authority carbon credit market. Local authorities were able to predict with accuracy the demand for energy, and therefore carbon, in their local areas.

++

Next Year (Year 3)

Government has again reduced the supply of carbon credits in the market by four per cent. This reduction will likely lead to increased competition for carbon credits, putting pressure on prices.

In Year 3, energy markets are widely predicted to be significantly less stable than in Years 1 and 2. Potential political instability in oil producing regions looks set to create uncertainty in the market. Added to this, talk of a major new entrant to the international energy markets persists. Energy supply could soon increase significantly.

These uncertainties seem set to cause price fluctuations in international energy markets. Energy price fluctuations would affect the UK carbon credit market. As a result, analysts are predicting with low levels of certainty that carbon credit prices are likely to rise to around £25 per tonne in Year 3. Government continues to anticipate that by the end of Year 5 the price of carbon credits will rise to around £35 per tonne.

Playing the Carbon Game

Start of Year – Analyst's Bulletin

++

Last Year (Year 3)

The estimated carbon credit price for Year 3 was £25. This estimate proved to be inaccurate. Prices of energy on the international markets proved to be unstable in Year 3. Continuing political instability in oil producing regions caused prices to rise early in the year. However, rumours of a major new entrant to the energy market proved accurate. Suddenly, long-term supplies of fossil fuels were greatly increased, leading to a sharp and sustained drop in prices.

This fall in prices led to a sharp increase in demand for energy. This greater demand translated into greater production of carbon dioxide across the UK. Almost all local authority predictions for how many carbon credits would be needed were too low. Competition for carbon credits on the market increased as councils vied for the limited supply of credits. As result prices for carbon credits rose. The actual price of a carbon credit in Year 3 was £29.70.

++

Next Year (Year 4)

Government has again reduced the supply of carbon credits in the market by four per cent. This reduction will likely lead to increased competition for carbon credits, pushing up prices.

In Year 4, energy prices are predicted to stabilise at lower levels than were seen in Years 1 and 2. However, there remains the possibility of the re-emergence of political instability in oil producing regions. This could again push up energy prices.

Analysts are predicting with low levels of certainty that carbon credit prices are likely to rise to around £33 in Year 4. Government has revised its estimate for the cost of a carbon credit by the end of Year 5. It now predicts that each will cost £40.

Playing the Carbon Game

Start of Year – Analyst's Bulletin

+++

Last Year (Year 4)

The estimated carbon credit price for Year 4 was £33. This estimate proved to be accurate, despite price instability in the international energy markets resulting from political instability in oil producing regions. Energy prices rose as future levels of supply increased.

Price increases led to a slightly lower demand for energy and hence slightly lower CO_2 production in England. Local authority forecasts of the need for carbon credits proved broadly accurate. The actual price of a carbon credit in Year 4 was £33.

+++

Next Year (Year 5)

Government has again reduced the supply of carbon credits in the market by four per cent. This reduction will likely lead to increased competition for carbon credits, pushing up prices.

Supply of and demand for energy are predicted to remain stable. However, the domestic political consequences of the drive to reduce carbon emissions are becoming more apparent. Analysts predict a growing resistance to CO_2 reduction measures. The consequences of this growing resistance might affect the operation of the market and hence the price of carbon credits.

Analysts are predicting with low levels of certainty that carbon credit prices are likely to rise to around £40 in Year 5. This is in line with previous Government predictions.

Appendix 6 *Carbon credit prices*

The research was designed to allow the annual prices of credits to fluctuate within predetermined boundaries. This was to give us the flexibility to vary prices according to the reaction of participants in the game. It also allowed the research to mimic the uncertainty of a real-world trading environment. We used to graph and table in Figure 21 to decide prices.

The orange line represents the rise in credit price year-on-year. The table highlights these annual prices in orange. As is shown, at the end of each year prices were increased to the maximum annual level allowed by the model.

During the simulation councils found cost-effectiveness a challenge. The rising cost of carbon credits firstly reflected the researcher's desire to give councils every opportunity to submit cost-effective packages. Price rises meant that schemes became more cost-effective over time. Secondly, it reflected the increasing scarcity of and competition for carbon credits. As is noted in the main report, overall cost-effectiveness was only achieved by year five of the simulation.

The starting and finishing prices for carbon credits were decided according to the existing data on the price of carbon permits and the social cost of carbon. The starting price at the beginning of year one of £18 per tonne of CO_2 was based on the period of peak prices experienced in the EU ETS in mid 2007 at the time of the project's construction. The finishing price at the end of year five was estimated to be £35-£40 per tonne. Stern accepts that his price of about £42 is at the high end of estimations.

---

67 Based on 16 September 2007 exchange rates

Figure 21 Carbon credit prices

Year	Increase on year one price	External shock (price drop)	No external shock	External shock (price rise)	Actual price
1	1	13.5	18	22.5	18
2	1.2	17.1	21.6	26.1	21.6
3	1.4	20.7	25.2	29.7	29.7
4	1.6	24.3	28.8	33.3	33.3
5	1.8	27.9	32.4	36.9	40

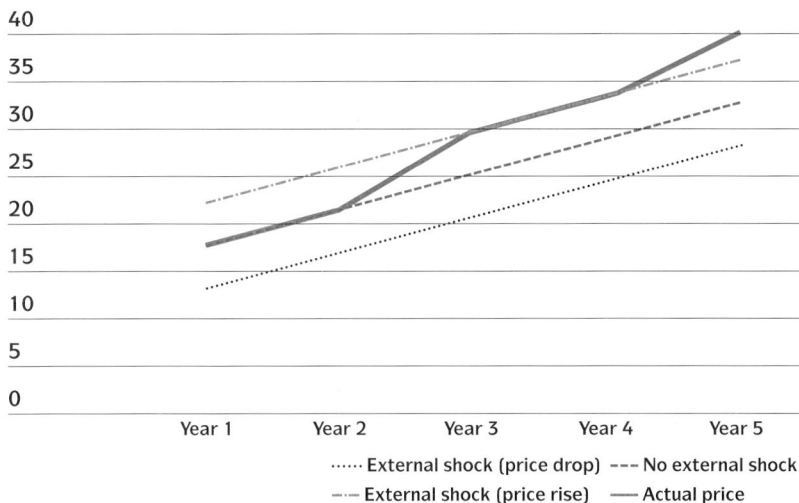

Appendix 7 *Complete list of suggested actions*

This appendix gives details of all the actions submitted throughout the research simulation.[68] They are largely unedited, except for information that would identify their origin. They are shown in descending order of claimed CO2 saving.

Description of CO2 reduction action	Self-assessed saving (tonnes CO2)	Estimated political impact[69]
Materials Exchange scheme for business (year one).	2,500,000	F
Materials Exchange scheme for business (year three). This handles a range of materials including construction and demolition waste. Major projects include schemes to reuse wood for DIY market.	2,500,000	F
Materials Exchange scheme for business (year three). This handles a range of materials including construction and demolition waste. Major projects include schemes to reuse wood for DIY market.	2,500,000	F
14 Anaerobic Digestion plants to process organic waste, producing energy from methane. Community Schemes, surplus to the grid.	1,050,000	F
50 per cent off a solar thermal panel for every household in the borough and 70 per cent off a solar PV installation.	550,000	U
Personalised carbon credits for all local residents, each allocated eight tonnes/year. Carbon credit card approach, where new meters are installed into houses, to clock up the amount of electricity utilised. Cars would also run on a similar device and flights would also be included within the scheme.	520,000	U
Electricity generating scheme linked to landfill sites extended to address remaining 4m tonnes of CO2 produced from such sites.	500,000	F
Electricity generating scheme linked to landfill sites extended to address remaining 4m tonnes of CO2 produced from such sites.	500,000	F

[68] Those actions judged to be unrealistic by experts or with incomplete data are included in this table. However, 25 of these 250 actions were removed from the final analysis

[69] Respondents were asked to mark each action as either favourable (U), neutral (N) or unfavourable (U)

Description of CO_2 reduction action	Self-assessed saving (tonnes CO_2)	Estimated political impact
Establish five District Energy Plants (CHP) run on wood chip from street trees, parks tress and residents tree waste – providing heat and water to 50 per cent of homes and businesses.	480,000	U
ESCO managing energy requirements of development in local Growth Area (37.5k homes, all built to be built at end of year five). Funded through Third Party Financing. (option for financing for the project without the authorities compromising own capital, thus leaving capital available for other priorities.)	375,000	U
ESCO managing energy requirements of development in a local Growth Area (37.5k homes, all built to be built at end of year five). Funded through Third Party Financing. (option for financing for the project without the authorities compromising own capital, thus leaving capital available for other priorities).	375,000	F
Developing a waste reduction, recycling and reusing campaign whereby details of how much commercial/industrial/construction/ demolition waste is closely monitoring (not presently done to a high standard). Items which are no longer needed by one company could be sold/ swapped for other items through the consortium.	302,100	F
Congestion charge for city centre and commuter routes backed up by low cost public transport system (including the expansion of the existing tram system). Congestion charge surplus pays for subsidised public transport. Designed to make public transport the best and only option.	290,000	N
Interest free loans to businesses to install solar PV or solar thermal.	200,000	U
Biomass (woodfuel) supply chain setup. A co-operative amongst key landowners linked to work around the county promoting use of biomass boilers.	200,000	F
Biomass energy schemes launched. Various including: woodchip CHP, energy from waste, and agricultural waste (through AD).	200,000	F
Biomass (woodfuel) supply chain setup. A co-operative amongst key landowners linked to work around the county promoting use of biomass boilers.	200,000	F
Biomass energy schemes launched. Various including: woodchip CHP, energy from waste, and agricultural waste (through AD).	200,000	F
Linking to Commitments in the LAA, joint local authority climate change strategy adopted. LSP created to deliver on targets mirroring the Government's own (60 per cent by 2050, with interim target of 26-32 per cent by 2020). Two per cent per annum.	143,000	F

Description of CO_2 reduction action	Self-assessed saving (tonnes CO_2)	Estimated political impact
Linking to Commitments in the LAA, joint local authority climate change strategy adopted. LSP created to deliver on targets mirroring the Government's own (60 per cent by 2050, with interim target of 26-32 per cent by 2020). Two per cent per annum.	143,000	F
Linking to Commitments in the LAA, joint local authority climate change strategy adopted. LSP created to deliver on targets mirroring the Government's own (60 per cent by 2050, with interim target of 26-32 per cent by 2020). Two per cent per annum.	143,000	F
Fossil fuel free zone in local city centre. Only vehicles allowed within run on alternative sources, including biofuels – mostly public transport.	125,000	F
Fossil fuel free zone in local city centre. Only vehicles allowed within run on alternative sources, including biofuels – mostly public transport.	125,000	F
Additional Park and Ride site.	100,000	N
Delivery of the Carbon Trust's 'Local Authority Carbon Management Programme'. Covers corporate buildings and rented housing stock. 30 per reduction in carbon emissions over five years.	100,000	F
'Cutting Your Carbon' Scheme. The scheme firstly ensures that adequate installer capacity exists in area by formulating a network of existing and new installers (through regional training opportunities). Householders are then asked to sign up to a 'Community Carbon Reduction Programme' and in doing so complete a Home Energy Check to ensure that all energy conservation and efficiency measures, such as insulation, are in place. Where a home could benefit from insulation and low energy light bulbs the council would facilitate a grant and provision of bulbs. Once through the 'Community Carbon Reduction Programme' system and all identified carbon saving measures have been employed the householder then is pre-qualified for the renewable energy carbon offsetting contribution. Householders then go through an initial self survey checklist to establish and ensure that their hypothetical choice of renewables concurs with what is practical and appropriate. Having done this the householder becomes eligible for the contribution and the network of installers fits the renewable energy technology.	100,000	F

Description of CO_2 reduction action	Self-assessed saving (tonnes CO_2)	Estimated political impact
Congestion scheme modified to be a road pricing scheme. Rather than focusing primarily on rush our traffic this has broadened to become a road pricing scheme for movement within the defined inner ring road. Managed in a similar way to the resident's parking scheme.	100,000	F
A further four Community CHP schemes.	100,000	F
Local Transport Plan has adopted a ten per cent reduction in emissions (by year five). A range of hard and soft measures developing (building on congestion charge and park and ride in previous years).	77,000	F
Local Transport Plan has adopted a ten per cent reduction in emissions (by year five). A range of hard and soft measures developing (building on congestion charge and park and ride in previous years).	77,000	F
Local Transport Plan has adopted a ten per cent reduction in emissions (by year five). A range of hard and soft measures developing (building on congestion charge and park and ride in previous years).	77,000	F
Energy efficiency consultancy programme for local businesses.	50,000	F
Energy efficiency installations in homes.	50,000	F
Continuation of energy efficiency consultancy programme for local businesses.	50,000	F
Continuation of energy efficiency installations in homes scheme.	50,000	F
Domestic waste recycling scheme that halves the amount of waste collected.	50,000	U
100,000 houses are to be built from 2006-2021 – ensure CHPs are incorporated into industrial, commercial and community heating.	50,000	F
Council incentive for energy efficiency in existing houses… the more energy efficient measures that are incorporated i.e. loft insulation – council tax is waived, as well as grants provided and advice given via the energy saving trust.	50,000	F
Creation of 'food hub' on outskirts of a local city. Major food distribution centre for movement of locally sourced food. Includes new rail links and freight distribution. Ecological budgeting technique has recognised that 'Food' as a sector has overall the biggest impact given its links to others such as waste and transport.	50,000	F

Description of CO$_2$ reduction action	Self-assessed saving (tonnes CO$_2$)	Estimated political impact
Continuation of energy efficiency consultancy programme for local businesses.	50,000	F
Continuation of energy efficiency installations in homes scheme.	50,000	F
Expansion of the council-wide ESCO.	50,000	F
School travel green bus scheme, no drive zones round schools.	50,000	N
In support of energy commitments in LAA run the Environmental Champions Scheme in a selected neighbourhood (1,000 homes).	40,000	U
In support of energy commitments in LAA run the Environmental Champions Scheme in a selected neighbourhood (1,000 homes). Year two roll out.	40,000	F
In support of energy commitments in LAA run the Environmental Champions Scheme in a selected neighbourhood (1,000 homes). Year two roll out.	40,000	F
An ESCO to promote the development and use of biomass for SMEs, schools and industry. Biomass sourced from within the city and later region by start-up company.	40,000	F
In support of energy commitments in LAA run the Environmental Champions Scheme in a selected neighbourhood (1,000 homes). Year four roll out.	40,000	F
Two Community CHP schemes.	40,000	F
In support of energy commitments in LAA run the Environmental Champions Scheme in a selected neighbourhood (1,000 homes). Year five roll out.	40,000	F
Year one of new Local Area Agreement on reducing carbon emissions. Continuation of grants and reductions on the installation of energy efficiency measures with the view of increasing the SAP rating in the borough.	35,000	F
Year two of new Local Area Agreement on reducing carbon emissions. Continuation of grants and reductions on the installation of energy efficiency measures with the view of increasing the SAP rating in the borough.	35,000	F
Year one of Efficient Homes scheme whereby homeowners are rewarded with £50 to have a residential energy audit – if their home scores above a certain threshold for efficiency they receive £50 off their council tax. If their homes require energy efficiency measures they receive £100 towards the installation of efficiency measures.	32,500	F

Description of CO_2 reduction action	Self-assessed saving (tonnes CO_2)	Estimated political impact
Year two of Efficient Homes scheme whereby homeowners are rewarded with £50 to have a residential energy audit – if their home scores above a certain threshold for efficiency they receive £50 off their council tax. If their homes require energy efficiency measures they receive £100 towards the installation of efficiency measures.	32,500	F
Major local development completed. Demolition and rebuild of 3,000 dwellings. Hydrogen cell CHP district heating scheme network. Includes school, 4,000 homes, community centre, church, shopping centre and leisure centre.	32,500	F
Rolling programme of free and subsidised roof and cavity wall insulation to private housing, (Public housing already done), delivered via a Community Interest Company set up to train and employ locals. Scheme subsidised by grant aid.	30,000	F
Pilot of Efficient Homes scheme whereby homeowners are rewarded with £50 to have a residential energy audit – if their home scores above a certain threshold for efficiency they receive £50 off their council tax. If their homes require energy efficiency measures they receive £100 towards the installation of efficiency measures.	30,000	F
Provide heat metering to 6,000 houses connected to community heating schemes. Reduces energy consumption by around 75 per cent.	30,000	N
Local Transport Plan restrict traffic increase.	25,000	U
Energy efficiency review of all council buildings – audits to ensure efficient building use (investigate use of buildings, outdated equipment, correctly setting timer clocks/programmers, space temperatures using buildings how they were designed to be used).	20,000	F
Full operation of the Frog island Bio MRF increasing the council's recycling rates to 47 per cent.	20,000	F
Establishment of an ESCO for the whole council.	20,000	F
Implementation of year one of the Local Area Agreement Stretch Target to implement the Warm Zones project to install insulation.	19,500	F
Implementation of year two of the Local Area Agreement Stretch Target to implement the Warm Zones project to install insulation.	19,500	F
Implementation of year three of the Local Area Agreement Stretch target to implement the Warm Zones project to install insulation.	19,500	F
Zero waste centre.	16,500	F

Description of CO_2 reduction action	Self-assessed saving (tonnes CO_2)	Estimated political impact
Zero waste centre.	16,500	F
Zero waste centre	16,500	F
Zero waste centre.	16,500	F
Commercial scale wind turbines within the council boundary. (Note: appropriate locations already identified by expert studies.) Five MW total. Energy generated supplied to needy in city at cost by arrangement with existing suppliers.	15,000	N
Additional support of the regional initiative on improving Domestic Energy Efficiency through incentives.	15,000	F
Introduce a carbon absorption and adaptation programme via strategic tree planting. Species to match climate change and shade buildings to reduce air conditioning requirements now and in future. Delivered via community groups and voluntary sector, BTCV etc.	15,000	F
Council wide lighting scheme to reduce energy used in council properties. Low energy lamps and automatic controls.	15,000	F
Household energy efficiency grant (run over five years for 50,000 homes).	13,000	U
Household energy efficiency grant (run over five years for 50,000 homes).	13,000	F
Household energy efficiency grant (run over five years for 50,000 homes).	13,000	F
Household energy efficiency grant (run over five years for 50,000 homes).	13,000	F
Household energy efficiency grant (run over five years for 50,000 homes).	13,000	F
Cut carbon emissions from the council buildings by five per cent.	12,000	F
Cut carbon emissions from the council buildings by five per cent.	12,000	F
Cut carbon emissions from the council buildings by five per cent.	12,000	F
Cut carbon emissions from the council buildings by five per cent.	12,000	F
Cut carbon emissions from the council buildings by five per cent.	12,000	F
Change from an organisation with a high IT carbon footprint to a very low IT carbon footprint. Done by modifying systems to reduce IT need, procuring low energy systems and equipment and educating staff. Reduce IT energy consumption by 50 per cent.	12,000	F

Description of CO₂ reduction action	Self-assessed saving (tonnes CO₂)	Estimated political impact
Completion of hydrogen fuelled CHP district heating system for Romford Town Centre's two major shopping centres and all public buildings.	10,924	N
Renewable energy grant scheme for community groups.	10,000	F
Transport scheme: Tax on vehicles travelling through town centres. Park and Ride centres to be situated on the out skirts of towns. Tax on vehicles redistributed through free train fares and bus fares, to encourage public transport.	10,000	U
A scheme to promote locally sourced products and services.	10,000	F
Additional support of regional initiative on improving Domestic Energy Efficiency through incentives.	10,000	F
Cut carbon emissions from the council buildings by ten per cent.	8,000	N
Continued ten per cent annual saving on carbon emissions from council buildings.	8,000	F
Congestion charge in a local city.	6,500	U
Congestion charge in a local city (year two).	6,500	U
Congestion charge in a local city (year three).	6,500	U
Street lighting switch off across to whole council area.	6,000	U
Opening of a new gasification plant removing 90,000 tonnes of waste from landfill per annum and generating 10MW energy per annum.	6,000	U
Implement Eco-Schools project (qualifies for £5k grant each). 50 schools per year target.	5,000	F
Implement Eco-Schools project (qualifies for £5k grant each). 50 schools per year target. Year two.	5,000	F
Implement Eco-Schools project (qualifies for £5k grant each). 50 schools per year target. Year two.	5,000	F
Low energy street lighting and traffic signals and renewable energy street furniture. High visibility projects to reduce the city's carbon emissions from street lighting.	5,000	F

Description of CO_2 reduction action	Self-assessed saving (tonnes CO_2)	Estimated political impact
Credit card system for local businesses whereby they have a maximum limit for carbon use… high energy intensive SMEs would have hand-holding advice to take them through the most cost-effective ways to reduce their impact. Competitions for the most innovative solutions… which would also improve business credentials and create new markets.	5,000	U
Implement Eco-Schools project (qualifies for £5k grant each). 50 schools per year target. Year three.	5,000	F
Area's recycling rates increase by a further five per cent to 52 per cent.	5,000	F
Implement Eco-Schools project (qualifies for £5k grant each). 50 schools per year target. Year five.	5,000	F
Kerbside recycling across the borough including publicity and education.	4,716	F
Kerbside recycling across the borough including publicity and education.	4,716	F
Conversion and new boilers where possible of 50 coal fired boilers to woodheat.	4,500	N
Supply 20 per cent of council energy from renewable sources	4,450	F
Supply 20 per cent of council energy from renewable sources	4,450	F
Supply 20 per cent of council energy from renewable sources	4,450	F
Roll out existing £1m 'invest to save' scheme, 50 per cent funded by the Carbon Trust.	3,400	N
Internal carbon management programme, business mileage reduction, facilities management projects, street lighting projects.	3,330	F
Clad every council housing block in solar PV (also is an effective insulation); each block to produce 250Kwh providing 100S of residents' electricity use and communal areas (lifts and lighting).	3,200	U
A tree planting scheme in support chiefly of Biodiversity Action Plan targets has been used to develop a carbon offsetting scheme to support local biodiversity projects. (130,000 trees per annum).	3,200	F
A tree planting scheme in support chiefly of Biodiversity Action Plan targets has been used to develop a carbon offsetting scheme to support local biodiversity projects. (130,000 trees per annum).	3,200	F

Description of CO₂ reduction action	Self-assessed saving (tonnes CO₂)	Estimated political impact
A tree planting scheme in support chiefly of Biodiversity Action Plan targets has been used to develop a carbon offsetting scheme to support local biodiversity projects. (130,000 trees per annum).	3,200	F
Improve the fabric of County Hall (per year).	3,000	F
Improve the fabric of County Hall (per year). Year two.	3,000	F
Improve the fabric of County Hall (per year). Year two.	3,000	F
Improve the fabric of County Hall (per year). Year two.	3,000	F
Year one of new Local Area Agreement on reducing carbon emissions. More installation of renewable energy technologies – wider remit to include non-public buildings and large scale renewable energy projects. These include the installation of three large wind turbines in a major local development. It will also include the installation of district heating systems.	3,000	F
Completed redevelopment of a local estate. Removal of 300 dwellings with a zero carbon development including a CHP district heating system run on local woodchip. This includes powering a new school and library through the district heating system.	3,000	F
Improve the fabric of County Hall (per year). Year five.	3,000	F
Year two of new Local Area Agreement on reducing carbon emissions. More installation of renewable energy technologies – wider remit to include non-public buildings and large scale renewable energy projects. It will also include the installation of district heating systems.	3,000	F
Develop staff awareness programme linked to 'Champions'.	2,500	N
Work to set up a system of river taxis (electric powered) to make better use of local waterways.	2,500	N
Year one of local carbon reduction incentive scheme for local residents with a loyalty card. Residents sign up to the scheme online and complete a monthly questionnaire on their energy and water use, car mileage, shopping habits, etc. Residents are rewarded with vouchers to restaurants, local events and local services.	2,500	F
Work to set up a transport system on an expanded river network to address flood risk but also to create an additional mode of electric powered transport.	2,500	N

Description of CO_2 reduction action	Self-assessed saving (tonnes CO_2)	Estimated political impact
Year two of local carbon reduction incentive scheme for local residents with a loyalty card. Residents sign up to the scheme online and complete a monthly questionnaire on their energy and water use, car mileage, shopping habits, etc. Residents are rewarded with vouchers to restaurants, local events and local services.	2,500	F
Implementation of 30 per cent renewables in major new developments and achievement of Code for Sustainable Homes Level 4.	2,375	N
Implementation of 30 per cent renewables in major new developments and achievement of Code for Sustainable Homes Level 4.	2,375	N
Implementation of 30 per cent renewables in major new developments and achievement of Code for Sustainable Homes Level 4.	2,375	N
Council sustainability festival 2011 with 20,000 visitors, each visitor at least receives an energy efficient light bulb and information on energy efficiency and climate change.	2,180	F
Carbon reduction communications campaign.	2,000	F
New household waste recycling centre.	2,000	N
The London Environment Centre, in partnership with the council, establish three businesses with Green Mark Level One and set up a Green Business Zone in a local industrial estate.	2,000	F
Council Carbon Business Partnership – pilot of an emissions trading network with the business parks in the area that are not captured in any other ETS scheme.	2,000	F
Implementation of 20 per cent renewables in major new developments and achievement of Code for Sustainable Homes Level 4.	1,900	N
Implementation of 20 per cent renewables in major new developments and achievement of Code for Sustainable Homes Level 4.	1,900	N
Planet 2010 with 15,000 visitors; each visitor at least receives an energy efficient light bulb and information on energy efficiency and climate change.	1,810	F
Council sustainability festival 2012 with 20,200 visitors; each visitor at least receives an energy efficient light bulb and information on energy efficiency and climate change.	1,800	F

Description of CO_2 reduction action	Self-assessed saving (tonnes CO_2)	Estimated political impact
Local environmental centre, in partnership with council, establish five more businesses with Green Mark accreditation.	1,500	F
Pilot of local carbon reduction incentive scheme for local residents with a loyalty card. Residents sign up to the scheme online and complete a monthly questionnaire on their energy and water use, car mileage, shopping habits, etc. Residents are rewarded with vouchers to restaurants, local events and local services.	1,500	F
Council's recycling rates increase by a further two per cent to 54 per cent.	1,500	F
Council-run environmental festival 2009 with 10,000 visitors, each visitor at least receives an energy efficient light bulb and information on energy efficiency and climate change.	1,340	F
Insulate ten per cent of existing domestic properties over a five year period; equates to 1,160 properties per year loft and cavity insulation (year one).	1,290	F
Insulate ten per cent of existing domestic properties over a five year period; equates to 1,160 properties per year loft and cavity insulation (year one).	1,290	F
Insulate ten per cent of existing domestic properties over a five year period; equates to 1,160 properties per year loft and cavity insulation (year one).	1,290	F
Insulate ten per cent of existing domestic properties over a five year period; equates to 1,160 properties per year loft and cavity insulation (year one).	1,290	F
'Mass Market Renewables Initiative', including a renewables showroom, domestic and business referral and quality assurance scheme.	1,235	F
Following the closure of one swimming pool and one ice rink in the council area, the new combined ice rink and swimming pool is completed. CHP system including a heat exchange between the two facilities. Zero carbon development.	1,200	N
New domestic waste fortnightly collection with door stepping waste minimisation campaign (recycling stays weekly as does green waste and compost collections).	1,000	U
Additional 1.8MW wind turbine built at a local manufacturing plant – planning permission awarded in 2005.	1,000	F

Description of CO$_2$ reduction action	Self-assessed saving (tonnes CO$_2$)	Estimated political impact
All council fleet converted to electric charged by solar PV at depot and solar roofs on vehicles	1,000	F
All council fleet converted to electric charged by solar PV at depot and solar roofs on vehicles	1,000	F
Local environmental centre, in partnership with the council, establishes five more businesses with Green Mark	1,000	F
Implementation of year two of the Local Area Agreement Stretch Target to refurbish and install renewable technology in public buildings – refurbishment of a local library to install a biomass boiler with combined heat and power to provide electricity and heating to the Library and heating to the adjacent Town Hall. Wood pellets.	800	F
50 per cent biofuel blend is available from the local fuelling station for the general public – increased uptake.	800	F
Implementation of year two of the Carbon Trust's carbon management programme.	700	F
Implementation of year three of the Carbon Trust's carbon management programme.	700	F
Reduce energy consumption by ten per cent in council buildings and street lighting based on energy consumption for council buildings and streetlighting and investment made as part of the LACM programme.	546	N
Existing 'Community Carbon Reduction Programme' rollout to businesses and schools.	525	F
Council's fleet to run on a 50 per cent biofuels mix from used cooking oil supplied by local partnership body.	500	F
Implementation of accommodation strategy review and implementation of New Ways of Working (hot-desking). Closing of two large oil-fired offices and an electric-heated gymnasium and assimilation of staff into existing buildings.	500	F
Reduce energy consumption by ten per cent in council buildings and street lighting based on energy consumption for council buildings and investment made as part of the LACM programme.	500	N
50 per cent biofuel blend is available from the local fuelling station to the general public.	500	F

Description of CO_2 reduction action	Self-assessed saving (tonnes CO_2)	Estimated political impact
Reduce energy consumption by ten per cent in council buildings and street lighting based on energy consumption for council buildings and investment made as part of the LACM programme.	500	N
Devising a local procurement strategy working out a guide for local business – Life Cycle Analysis, working with local businesses, providing advice and ensuring they only procure goods which are locally sourced.	500	F
Three new zero carbon schools built to replace six schools that have been closed and demolished. This is due to falling enrolment levels for primary schools.	500	F
Reduce energy consumption by ten per cent in council buildings and street lighting based on energy consumption for council buildings and investment made as part of the LACM programme.	500	N
Reduce energy consumption by ten per cent in council buildings and street lighting based on energy consumption for council buildings and investment made as part of the LACM programme.	500	N
Year one of the council's internal carbon trading scheme. Each service is allocated a set level of carbon emission permits with the aim of a ten per cent reduction in energy consumption in year one. Services exceeding their targets can sell their permits to other services, and visa versa.	450	N
Installation of renewable technologies including wind power, solar hot water and photovoltaics in ten schools.	400	F
Council-run environmental festival 2008 with 10,000 visitors; each visitor at least receives an energy efficient light bulb and information on energy efficiency and climate change.	399	F
Insulate ten per cent of existing domestic properties over a five year period, equates to 1,160 properties per year loft and cavity insulation (year one).	352	F
Council buildings – installation of software to switch off PCs at night/weekend and daytime protocols.	350	F
Implementation of year one of the Carbon Trust's carbon management programme.	333	F
Emissions-based parking charges.	300	F
Establishing a borough wide commercial recycling service. Each tonne collected saves approx one tonne CO_2.	300	F

Description of CO_2 reduction action	Self-assessed saving (tonnes CO_2)	Estimated political impact
'Energy Futures' project in high schools after trials in primary schools showed potential carbon savings of 30 per cent. Engage with 40 schools this year.	300	F
Implementation of year two Sustainable Procurement Action Plan in partnership with a consultancy.	300	F
'Energy Futures' project in high schools after trials in primary schools showed potential carbon savings of 30 per cent. Engage with 40 schools this year.	300	F
Implementation of year three Sustainable Procurement Action Plan in partnership with a consultancy. Part of year three implementation is that all corporate contractors required to submit a carbon reduction strategy as part of the procurement process, with information on their carbon emission record.	300	F
'Energy Futures' project in high schools after trials in primary schools showed potential carbon savings of 30 per cent. Engage with 40 schools this year.	300	F
'Energy Futures' project in high schools after trials in primary schools showed potential carbon savings of 30 per cent. Engage with 40 schools this year.	300	F
Replacement of six oil-fired boilers in six schools with biomass boilers. The boilers will initially be powered using pellets.	272	F
Replacement of six oil-fired boilers in six schools with biomass boilers. The boilers will initially be powered using pellets.	272	F
Reduce council waste stream by 30 per cent, increase recycling by 20 per cent, increase spend on green procurement (including recycled content materials).	270	F
Installation of renewable technologies including wind power, solar hot water and photovoltaics in six schools.	240	F
Facilitate increased car club provision.	200	F
Rigorous enforcement of bus lanes (removing parked vehicles, etc).	200	F
Local inter-council partnership body secure implementation of three partnership travel plans for local shopping centres and industrial estates.	200	F
All biomass boilers now fired with wood chip from local sources. Council-owned land used for coppicing. Reduced transport and processing requirements.	200	F

Description of CO_2 reduction action	Self-assessed saving (tonnes CO_2)	Estimated political impact
Developing a centralised 'consortium of local businesses' good practice guide for local businesses and working with them to reduce their ecological footprint, working in partnership with a local university and other colleges, so new innovative technological ideas are shared and discussed, and businesses wok together.	200	F
Year two of the council internal carbon trading scheme. Each service is allocated a set level of carbon emission permits with the aim of a five per cent reduction in energy consumption in year two. Services exceeding their targets can sell their permits to other services, and visa versa.	200	F
New supermarket and residential development includes CHP and heat exchange between refrigeration units and housing developments, as well as two wind turbines.	180	f
Year three of the council internal carbon trading scheme. Each service is allocated a set level of carbon emission permits with the aim of a five per cent reduction in energy consumption in year two. Services exceeding their targets can sell their permits to other services, and visa versa.	180	F
Installation of a 2MW turbine in a local park under the PfR scheme	150	U
Implementation of year three of the Local Area Agreement Stretch Target to refurbish and install renewable technology in public buildings – solar hot water heating and photovoltaic array at three major leisure centres (a sports centre).	150	N
Five per cent biodiesel in all council fleet. All diesel fleet.	139	F
Five per cent biodiesel in all council fleet. All diesel fleet.	139	F
Five per cent biodiesel in all council fleet. All diesel fleet.	139	F
Five per cent biodiesel in all council fleet. All diesel fleet.	139	F
Council buildings energy awareness campaign with staff – ten per cent reduction in energy use.	101	F
Council's fleet to run on a 20 per cent biofuels mix from used cooking oil supplied by a locally, publicly funded partnership organisation.	100	F
Implementation of year two of the Local Area Agreement Stretch Target to refurbish and install renewable technology in public buildings – small wind turbine on two council buildings.	100	N
Car parking zone charges linked with vehicle emissions.	100	U

Description of CO₂ reduction action	Self-assessed saving (tonnes CO₂)	Estimated political impact
Council's fleet to run on a 20 per cent biofuels mix from used cooking oil supplied by a locally, publicly-funded partnership organisation.	67	F
Local council partnership secure implementation of work-based travel plans with the all local public sector bodies.	60	F
Retrofit of five council buildings to upgrade to CHP biomass boilers/install new heating controls/ install solar thermal and solar PV 40KWP.	56	F
School travel plans resulted in an additional modal shift of five per cent based on 2008/09 figures.	50	F
Local inter-council partnership body secure implementation of three work-based travel plans with major local employers.	50	F
Implementation of year three of the Local Area Agreement Stretch Target to refurbish and install renewable technology in public buildings – solar hot water heating and photovoltaics on a new depot and photovoltaics on a local theatre.	50	N
Charging non-essential car users for council-provided parking spaces provides additional incentive for modal shift.	50	F
Local council partnership secure implementation of work-based travel plans at local Industrial Park and other major local employers.	50	F
Borough-wide green collection available fortnightly.	50	N
Year one of new Local Area Agreement on reducing carbon emissions. Installation of 60 solar hot water heating units into council stock.	30	F
Year two of new Local Area Agreement on reducing carbon emissions. Installation of 60 solar hot water heating units into council stock.	30	F
Year three of the council's staff travel plan resulting in a furthera modal shift of six per cent. Adoption of home working policy reduces daily travel to work by ten per cent.	25	F
Implementation of year one of the Local Area Agreement Stretch Target to refurbish a local library.	20	F
All schools to begin implementation of school travel plans resulting in an average modal shift of five per cent based on 2006/07 figures.	18	F
Year three of council's staff travel plan resulting in a further modal shift of two per cent. Adoption of home working policy reduces daily travel to work by additional five per cent.	18	F

Description of CO_2 reduction action	Self-assessed saving (tonnes CO_2)	Estimated political impact
Moving of depot from one location to another, resulting in reduced travel distance of five per cent per annum.	17	F
Implementation of year one of the Local Area Agreement Stretch Target to install solar hot water heating into 30 council stock.	15	F
Implementation of year three of the Local Area Agreement Stretch Target to install solar hot water heating into 30 council stock.	15	F
Year two of council's staff travel plan resulting in a further modal shift of ten per cent.	15	F
Implementation of year three of the Local Area Agreement Stretch Target to install solar hot water heating into 30 council stock.	15	F
School travel plans resulted in an additional modal shift of three per cent based on 2008/09 figures.	15	F
Ten per cent of households to be supplied with compost bins; investment from Waste & Resources Action Programme (WRAP).	14	N
10% of household to be supplied with compost bins; investment from WRAP.	14	N
School travel plans resulted in an additional modal shift of two per cent based on 2008/09 figures.	12	F
Implementation of the council's staff travel plan resulting in a modal shift of eight per cent.	2	F
Planting 200 additional trees as part of a new community forest programme.	2	F
Planting of 200 additional trees in a new community forest.	2	F
Planting of 200 additional trees as part of a new community forest.	2	F
Adoption of the Climate Change Strategy and Sustainable Energy Strategy Action Plan.	0	F
Master planning for the replacement of 1,000 pre-fab 1930s homes with 3,000 zero-carbon homes and a zero-carbon biomass-powered school.	0	F
Planting of 100 trees as part of a new community forest programme.	0	F
Potential for district heating schemes in the borough are mapped.	0	F
Five small biodiesel plants created within the county using Koldron technology (currently most of the waste vegetable oil collected in the county is exported to Germany to be made into biodiesel). Local distribution to forecourts within county setup.		F

Description of CO_2 reduction action	Self-assessed saving (tonnes CO_2)	Estimated political impact
Materials exchange scheme for business. In development.	?	F
Woodfuel infrastructure. In development.	?	N
Fossil fuel free zone in a local city. Only vehicles allowed within run on alternative sources, including biofuels – mostly public transport	?	F
Creation of 'food hub' on outskirts of a local city. Major food distribution centre for movement of locally-sourced food. Includes new rail links.	?	N
Establishment of the council 'carbon neutral fund'. Developers are charged £250 for each tonne of carbon their development will emit on an annual basis. This fund will be used for the installation of energy efficient technologies and renewable energies throughout the borough.	?	N
CHPs designed to utilise food and garden waste – so diverted from landfill and methane prevented.	?	N
Year two of the council 'carbon neutral fund'. Developers are charged £250 for each tonne of carbon their development will emit on an annual basis. This fund will be used for the installation of energy efficient technologies and renewable energies throughout the borough.	?	F
Biomass energy schemes launched. Various, including woodchip CHP, energy from waste, agricultural waste (through AD). To be developed.	?	N

Appendix 8 *Domestic microgeneration and planning*

In August 2007, NLGN published a paper that outlined a package of recommendations to encourage a faster and more widespread adoption of domestic microgeneration. This is included in this appendix. It examines the Government's current proposals for reforming the planning system to promote domestic microgeneration and the principles on which these reforms are based. It goes on to propose that frontline councillors should direct neighbourhood-level consulation processes aimed at creating local regulations more permissive than national minimum standards. Legislation on local planning flexibility should be amended to reflect this new level of public probity.

Flexibilities alone are not enough; incentives are neccessary. To make adoption more likely, local authorities could introduce tax breaks and local finance for those who install small-scale generation technology. Central government could give local authorities incentives to promote microgeneration through a cost-neutral performance grant that would reward those who improve most quickly. The prize is a future in which microgeneration plays its full role in tackling climate change.

The text of the full paper follows overleaf.

1 Introduction

The planning system is central to the fight against climate change. Government is taking steps to reform the rules and encourage householders to take action to reduce their environmental footprints.

The Department of Communities Local Government (DCLG) recently published a consultation document on loosening regulatory restrictions on domestic microgeneration in England. The proposals would make it easier for householders to install solar panels, wind turbines and other microgeneration equipment on their own houses without needing planning consent, as long as the impact on neighbouring properties was minimal.

The findings of an earlier review underpin Government's current proposals. The Householder Development Consents Review (HDCR)[A1] found that the planning system failed to reflect the principle that planning consent would only be needed where the development had a significant impact beyond the property. The report concluded that this situation was not satisfactory. Government is addressing this concern and embedding the principle across the planning regime. DCLG hopes that its plans will balance acceptable impact with protecting *'residential amenity'*.[A2]

This 'impact principle' is at the heart of the Barker Review of land use. For Barker, planning consent would only be needed in cases of *'non-marginal third-party impact'*.[A3] The recent Planning White Paper re-asserts the need to remove low-impact developments from the planning system.

For domestic microgeneration, a more flexible planning regime could have big effects on attempts to tackle climate change. Research from the Energy Savings Trust shows that domestic microgeneration could provide 30 to 40 per cent of the UK's energy needs by 2050.[A4] Stern supports this finding; for him, microgeneration can be a part of tackling the worst impacts of climate change.[A5]

The impending Planning Bill, as well as other non-legislative reforms that Government is making to the planning system, will be vital in deciding for years

A1 Published in January 2005

A2 Department for Communities and Local Government, *Changes to Permitted Development – Consultation Paper 1:Permitted Development Rights for Householder Microgeneration* (April 2007), p 9

A3 Kate Barker, *Barker Review of Land Use Planning Final Report* (December 2006), p 118

A4 Energy Saving Trust, *Potential for Microgeneration: Study and Analysis – Executive Summary* (November 2005)

A5 Sir Nicholas Stern, *Review Report on the Economics of Climate Change* (October 2006), p 384

to come how well the planning regime aids the fight against climate change. As one of the first pieces of reform to the system, the proposed changes to the rules for domestic microgeneration will influence the course of wider reform. Ensuring that new regulations promote as fast and wide a take-up as possible is therefore important.

The first section examines the proposals put forward by Government and the principles on which they are based. The second outlines how more ambitious reforms might help to provoke a more widespread and faster adoption of domestic microgeneration technology.

2 Lowering barriers

The proposals to reform the Town and Country Planning (General Permitted Development) Order 199 (GPDO) are intended to reduce the proportion of domestic microgeneration installations that need planning consent. With these reforms, Government aims to strike an appropriate balance between a wide take-up of domestic microgeneration and the protection of neighbours, the environment and the wider community from negative effects.

The impact principle

The January 2005 ODPM Householder Development Consents Review (HDCR) found that the then system for granting planning consent and for deciding what is permitted development was not appropriate. Most importantly, the planning system did not properly distinguish between impactful and impact-free development, tending to focus on the volume of developments rather than their effects. Despite the limited scope of the review, Government now sees these findings as applicable to domestic microgeneration.

Government seeks to define acceptable impact on an England-wide basis by creating quantified thresholds for noise pollution and visual impact. Different thresholds are to be created for different kinds of microgeneration equipment. If a piece of equipment falls below the threshold, it will be considered permitted development. If it falls above, it will require a planning consent.

The England-wide impact thresholds would be defined as follows:[A6]

A6 DCLG, *Changes to Permitted Development – Consultation Paper 1:Permitted Development Rights for Householder Microgeneration* (April 2007), p 28

Solar on buildings	Permitted for the roof and walls unless it protrudes more than 150 mm above roof plane.
Solar stand alone	Permitted if less than 4 metres height. At least 5 metres to any boundary. Area of array a maximum 9m².
Ground source heat pumps	Permitted.
Air source heat pumps	Permitted if – internal noise <30dB, external noise <40dB, "garden" noise <40dB.
Water source heat pumps	Permitted.
Wind turbines on buildings	Permitted if <3m above ridge (including the blade) and diameter of blades <2m. Also internal noise <30dB, external noise <40dB, "garden" noise <40dB. Up to 4 turbines on buildings >15m (as with antennas). Vibration <0.5mm/s.
Wind turbines (stand alone)	Permitted if <11m (including the blade) high and diameter of blades <2m. At least 12m from a boundary. Also internal noise <30dB, external noise <40dB, "garden" noise <40dB. Vibration <0.5mm/s.
Bio Mass	Permitted – Limit of Flue height 1m above ridge.
Combined heat and power	Permitted – Limit of Flue height 1m above ridge.
Hydro	No change.

Exemptions

Despite the commitment to a uniform approach to assessing impact, the proposed changes go on to recommend local variability in the application of the new regulations. The proposals recognise that, *'the type of development should not only reflect what the development is, but where it is.'*[A7]

Government suggests that the requirement for planning consent will not be relaxed in Conservation Areas and World Heritage Sites. In these areas, the following thresholds would continue to apply:[A8]

A7 DCLG, *Changes to Permitted Development – Consultation Paper 1:Permitted Development Rights for Householder Microgeneration* (April 2007), p11
A8 DCLG, *Changes to Permitted Development – Consultation Paper 1:Permitted Development Rights for Householder Microgeneration* (April 2007), p28

Solar on buildings	Permitted as normal, except on principal elevation fronting a highway.
Solar stand alone	Permitted as normal except in front of principal elevation.
Ground source heat pumps	Permitted.
Air source heat heat pumps	Permitted as normal except on principal elevation fronting a highway.
Water source heat pumps	Permitted.
Wind turbines on buildings	Not permitted.
Wind turbines (stand alone)	Permitted as normal except in front of principal elevation.
Bio Mass	Flues permitted as normal except on principal elevation fronting a highway.
Combined heat and power	Flues permitted as normal except on principal elevation fronting a highway.
Hydro	No change

Also, specific permission would still be needed to make alterations to listed buildings. National government also plans to issue guidance to householders and local authorities on the implementation of these regulations.

The success of these reforms will have an effect on what happens in the rest of the planning system. The wider reform process is underway, with the consultation attached to the recent Planning White Paper asking how such future regulations for industrial and commercial buildings should be structured.[9]

3 Recommendations for reform

A new role for neighbourhood decisions-making?

A contradiction lies at the heart of Government's proposals. On the one hand, the paper embraces the principle in the earlier review of householder planning regulations, that, 'the national GPDO provides all householders with a level of certainty that should be retained'.[10]

A9 DCLG, *Planning for a Sustainable Future, Consultation* (May 2007), Q 38, p21

A10 DCLG, *Householder Development Consents Review: Implementation of Recommendations* (May 2007), p 16

However, Conservation Areas and World Heritage Sites would be subject to tighter regulations; small wind turbines, for example, would not count as permitted development in these areas.

The concept of local variation is already embraced in the planning regime. Local Development Orders (LDOs), introduced as an optional part of Local Development Frameworks in 2004, give local planning authorities powers to tailor regulations. The orders allow for an extension of permitted development rights in defined areas, or even the abolition of planning restrictions where appropriate. In the present system, the Secretary of State retains powers of amendment and veto over any LDO.

Government should choose to expand the potential of LDOs and make local variability in regulations a central feature of the planning system. To do this, Whitehall could attempt to work with individual planning authorities to define acceptable impact on a neighbourhood-by-neighbourhood basis, constantly updating definitions and regulations to cater for a fluid landscape. But it would be a huge task.

Instead, frontline councillors, working with citizens, should be empowered to shape LDOs according to local opinion. Constructing a system that adequately caters for local public opinion and ensures that plans are in the public interest would remove the need for the Secretary of State to reserve veto powers. This approach could lead to a faster and more widespread adoption of domestic microgeneration technology. This would mean that citizens living in Conservation Areas and World Heritage Sites could also be given the level of influence required to relax the barriers to domestic microgeneration where such action was warranted in the judgement of frontline councillors.

Delivering neighbourhood variability

Changes to the operation of LDOs would call for legislation in the upcoming Planning Bill. Changes could be as follows:

- Repeal the Secretary of State's powers to amend, veto and revoke LDOs.

- Introduce a new requirement to ensure that any plans were tested against the local public interest in those areas directly affected by new local arrangements.

A new LDO would almost certainly reduce the number of applications that a planning department would have to process by lowering the bar on permitted development. At a time when there is increasing pressure on planners to process quickly applications for planning consent, this would be an added advantage.

Local authorities would be required to demonstrate that neighbourhood plans to widen the terms of permitted development were in the public interest. To do so, local authorities should do the following:

* Charge frontline councillors with the responsibility for new neighbourhood regulations that would define a higher tolerable impact than the national minimum standards set-out in the reformed GPDO.

* Charge frontline councillors with the responsibility for convening neighbourhood forums to test proposed new neighbourhood regulations against local opinion in the affected neighbourhood.

* After the conclusion of the forum, frontline councillors would be responsible for making the subsequent decision on whether to extend permitted development taking into account neighbourhood opinion. The frontline councillor would not be bound by the forum's decision.

This approach would need a mechanism for reviewing neighbourhood arrangements. Local authorities could require that frontline councillors review neighbourhood regulations on an annual basis. A neighbourhood forum convened to review existing neighbourhood regulations should be different to the one to debate possible new regulations. If existing regulations and new proposals are both rejected then the new GPDO standards should apply.

This approach would be in line with Government's aspiration expressed in the recent Local Government White Paper to, *'involve citizens directly in designing, delivering or assessing a service.'*[A11] Protests by residents about particular installations should be addressed at the neighbourhood level by frontline councillors.

Incentivising microgeneration

To make microgeneration installations more attractive to local citizens, local authorities could introduce local tax incentives:

A11 DCLG, *Strong and Prosperous Communities: The Local Government White Paper* (October 2006) , p32

- Local authorities could introduce substantial Council Tax rebates for those households that install domestic microgeneration equipment not requiring planning consent.

If local authorities find a rebate approach too onerous, there are alternative incentives: local authorities could help to make the financial benefits of microgeneration more tangible to householders from the date of installation. The financial benefit of installing photovoltaic solar panels, for example, would generally be realised over a number of years. The long-term nature of the investment can dissuade householders from making the necessary capital investment.

- To cater for this, local authorities could introduce loans for householders to pay for micro-generation installations to be repaid over the lifetime of the equipment. Such loans to householders could be a more manageable commitment for local authorities to bear, even if interest free or low interest. Legislation to allow such loan arrangements should be enacted to provide clarity for authorities.

These amendments alone would be unlikely to persuade English local authorities to spontaneously introduce variable planning regulations. Also, Council Tax rebates might undermine a local authority's willingness to pursue new neighbourhood regulations. Government could give a new set of incentives to persuade local authorities to make promoting domestic microgeneration a priority:

- Central government could introduce a performance grant for the local authority allocated on the basis of the amount of sustainable electricity generated per-house through microgeneration in the local authority area:

  - The terms of the performance grant could be varied area-by-area. Grants could be awarded on the basis of rate of improvement rather than absolute levels of sustainable energy generated

  - This microgeneration performance grant should be measured in the new Comprehensive Area Assessment (CAA) regime and funding routed through the second wave of Local Area Agreements (LAA)

  - This performance grant could be designed to be more valuable than the cost of Council Tax rebates where the local authority reaches and/or exceeds the target negotiated through the LAA

- This performance grant could form a part of the local government grants regime and be cost neutral for central government, where the cost of rewarding successful authorities is offset by a mild penalty for poor performance

4 Conclusion

The reforms to the regulations on the permitted developments for domestic microgeneration presented in the consultation are a demonstration of Government's renewed commitment to planning playing its part in building a sustainable energy infrastructure. Lowering the barriers to householders installing wind turbines, solar panels and similar equipment will go some way to realising the potential of microgeneration.

Central government could choose to try and cater for all kinds of variation in new regulations, but attempting this could turn into a never-ending task. Instead, Government could create a new system that would encourage local authorities to make the best use of diversity to create a new system from the bottom-up.

In a new system, the GPDO should be reformed as outlined in the consultation. This would set England-wide standards for permitted development for household microgeneration. Changes to the rules on LDOs would then further empower local authorities to allow more permitted development in certain areas without needing tacit permission from the Secretary of State.

In this new system, local authorities would be required to demonstrate that LDO plans were in the public interest. This would require neighbourhood level consultation and debate, giving citizens a powerful voice. Frontline councillors would be at the heart of this process, supported by local officers. Listening to the voices of local people in this way would ensure that 'residential amenity' was protected as defined by residents. Council tax rebates and capital loans for householders that install domestic microgeneration equipment would incentivise local people to engage in the process.

Despite the potential strengths of such a system, it is unlikely that all local authorities would spontaneously take advantage of new flexibilities. Central government should introduce a cost neutral performance grant that would raise the issue up councils' priority lists while at the same time compensating councils for lowering their tax bases. CAAs and LAAs would be essential in measuring progress and allocating funding.

This system would empower local citizens and frontline representatives to take ownership of the impact of domestic microgeneration in their neighbourhoods. For the whole of the state, the prize is a sustainable future where domestic microgeneration plays its full role.

Kirklees

Kirklees Council has taken the lead on climate change for many years, setting ambitious emissions reduction targets, producing demonstration renewable energy projects (including the UK's largest solar village) and raising awareness.

Kirklees Council has also pledged to be 'a beacon for green living' as part of its Green Ambition. In 2005 Kirklees achieved a 34 per cent reduction in CO_2 emissions from a 1990 baseline, and have set another target of reducing emissions by a further 30 per cent by 2020. Their civic centre now has the first two 6kW wind turbines installed on the roof of a council building in the UK, along with 220 solar PV panels and 48m² of solar thermal panels.

Kirklees Council have recently launched the country's biggest Warm Zone, providing every resident in the district (regardless of income) with free loft and cavity wall insulation, saving an estimated 17,000 tonnes of CO_2 per year.

For more information, please visit **www.kirklees.gov.uk**

Kirklees
COUNCIL

Serco

Serco is an international service company which combines commercial know-how with a deep public service ethos.

We improve services by managing people, processes, technology and assets more effectively. We advise policy makers, design innovative solutions, integrate systems and – most of all – deliver to the public.

Serco supports governments, agencies and companies who seek a trusted partner with a solid track-record of providing assured service excellence. Our people offer operational, management and consulting expertise across a wide spectrum of industry sectors including local government.

Our local government services include waste management, street-scene, landscaping, building maintenance, leisure services, ICT, e-gov solutions and consulting services.

For more information, please visit **www.serco.com**

serco

Please complete both sides of this order form and return it with your payment to **Central Books, 99 Wallis Road, London E9 5LN**. Alternatively, you may email your order information to **info@nlgn.org.uk** or visit **www.nlgn.org.uk**

Your order	£ per copy	Quantity
Carbon Footprints, Local Steps: How local government can rise to the climate change challenge	£15+p&p	
Capital Ideas: Financing future local economic development	£17+p&p	
Conservatives and Localism: An NLGN series of party pamphlets	£12+p&p	
Redesigning Regionalism: Leadership and accountability in England's regions	£15+p&p	
The Politics of Shared Services: What are the underlying barriers to a more successful shared services agenda?	£12+p&p	
Schools of Thought: How local authorities drive improved outcomes in education	£12+p&p	
Lib Dems and Localism: An NLGN series of party pamphlets	£12+p&p	
Labour and Localism: An NLGN series of party pamphlets	£12+p&p	
Views of the City: Can city-regions find their place?	£12+p&p	
Evolution and Devolution in England How regions strengthen our towns and cities	£20+p&p	
Order subtotal	£	
Postage and packing (£1.25 x number of publications)	£	
Order total	£	

Deliver to (block capitals please)

Name

Job title

Organisation/company/institution

Address

Postcode   County

Telephone   Fax

Email

Invoice to if different from the delivery information above

Name

Job title

Organisation/company/institution

Address

Postcode   County

Telephone   Fax

Email

Method of payment

Please invoice my organisation/company/institution on account **or**

I enclose a cheque for £   payable to *Central Books Ltd* **or**

Please charge my credit/debit card as follows

Visa   Mastercard   Switch/Maestro   Delta

Card number

Amount £   Issue no (Debit cards only)

Expiry date   Start date (Switch/Maestro only)

Name on card (CAPS)   Signature x

Orders will normally be processed within five working days –
if your order is very urgent, please state your delivery deadline below